Peace, Love, Happiness

Sandra M. Lowe

In the Beginning

Sandra M. Lowe

BALBOA
PRESS

A DIVISION OF HAY HOUSE

Copyright © 2013 Sandra M. Lowe.

All rights reserved. No part of this book may be used or reproduced by any means, graphic, electronic, or mechanical, including photocopying, recording, taping or by any information storage retrieval system without the written permission of the publisher except in the case of brief quotations embodied in critical articles and reviews.

Balboa Press books may be ordered through booksellers or by contacting:

Balboa Press
A Division of Hay House
1663 Liberty Drive
Bloomington, IN 47403
www.balboapress.com
1-(877) 407-4847

Because of the dynamic nature of the Internet, any web addresses or links contained in this book may have changed since publication and may no longer be valid. The views expressed in this work are solely those of the author and do not necessarily reflect the views of the publisher, and the publisher hereby disclaims any responsibility for them.

The author of this book does not dispense medical advice or prescribe the use of any technique as a form of treatment for physical, emotional, or medical problems without the advice of a physician, either directly or indirectly. The intent of the author is only to offer information of a general nature to help you in your quest for emotional and spiritual well-being. In the event you use any of the information in this book for yourself, which is your constitutional right, the author and the publisher assume no responsibility for your actions.

Any people depicted in stock imagery provided by Thinkstock are models, and such images are being used for illustrative purposes only.
Certain stock imagery © Thinkstock.

ISBN: 978-1-4525-7258-1 (sc)
ISBN: 978-1-4525-7256-7 (hc)
ISBN: 978-1-4525-7257-4 (e)

Library of Congress Control Number: 2013907392

Printed in the United States of America.

Balboa Press rev. date: 6/7/2013

For my family

Spirit is in a state of grace forever.
Your reality is only spirit.
Therefore you are in a state of grace forever.

—A Course in Miracles

CONTENTS

Foreword xi
A Note to Readers xiii
Glossary xv
Map of Lake Superior Provincial Park and area xvii

Led by Grace

Introduction 1

In the Beginning

My First Steps 9
Crossing My Bridges 17
The Body's Flaws, The Spirit's Perfection 23
A Pot of Gold 29
Reflections 33
What Looks Easy Is Not Always So 37
A Stranger 41
My Plans for Salvation 47
Getting Naked, Experiencing Love 53
My View from Three Eyes 61
The City of Gold 69
Never Forgotten, Just Not Remembered 79
Eaten Alive 83
Painting Our Self-Portrait 89
Wanted 99
Cleansed of My Gold 107
My Eagle's Spirit Breath 115
Teachings of the Dogwood 119

Unlocking My Soul	129
My Heart's Secret Garden	139
My Miracle of a Dove	145
Meeting Jesus	153
At the Center of the Wagon Wheel	163
Chains of the Body, Freedom of the Soul	169
Answering the Call	175
Afterword	180
Acknowledgments	181
Permissions	182
Bibliography	183
About the Author	185

Foreword

I met Sandra in 2000 after I moved to Wawa to set up a private practice for massage therapy and Reiki treatments.

Reiki (Rei means "life force," and ki means "energy" in Japanese) is an ancient, hands-on healing practice. It originated in Tibet thousands of years ago and was rediscovered in the late 1800s by Dr. Mikao Usui, a Japanese Buddhist. In this gentle, safe healing practice, the Reiki practitioner is a conduit for universal life force energy. The client must be open to receiving this energy, which will only go to where it is needed, be it for emotional, mental, spiritual, or physical healing.

Sandra initially attended my home business for a massage therapy session. However, after this first treatment, I intuitively sensed that she might benefit from energy work. When I introduced her to Reiki, she elected to try it. She seemed a little apprehensive in the beginning, but after a couple of sessions, she soaked in the energy like a sponge and scheduled weekly Reiki sessions. She was fascinated by the many visions/meditations that would arise as she relaxed more deeply into the treatments. She soon started journaling after the sessions, and she has intuitively analyzed these visions to uncover her authentic self. On this path to inner peace, she courageously and openly shared many feelings and profound spiritual insights with me as they occurred over the three years I was in Wawa.

The *Led by Grace* collection is Sandra's inspiring story, beginning after her first session of Reiki. It is a journey of self-discovery, freed from the bondages of fear to an opened heart of love, transforming from her cocoon to soaring as a beautiful butterfly in the world, a true marvel of bravery. A story you will never forget—may it transform you and your world.

In light and love,
Anna Marie Bougie,
North Bay, Ontario

A Note to Readers

In this book, capitalized words express the essential attributes of "All That Is." You will see many words—God, Grace, Spirit, Oneness, Source Energy, Infinite—I use to name that which is nameless. Capitalized words such as our Self, our Being, our Nature, our Essence, express this same God-Presence within us.

Words of emotion or "conditions" such as Love, Peace, Patience, Truth are capitalized to incorporate or indicate the aspects of "All That Is" in the meaning of the word.

A capitalized word holds great meaning.

Certain lower case words have significance as well. My "self" reflects the belief that we are our bodies, separate from each other and from this God-Presence. Similarly, "who we are" recognizes this same belief while "Who we are" identifies us as Grace.

Glossary

Animal Medicine: In Native American teachings, "medicine" is anything that deepens our connection to Spirit and to all life. Animals offer such medicine. Each animal, based on its habits and behaviors, is associated with a lesson or concept to help in our healing of body, mind, and spirit (Sams and Carson, 1999, 10).

Camino de Santiago de Compostela: Translated "The Way of St. James" and dating back to the tenth century, the Camino is a network of ancient pilgrimage routes originating from all over Europe to the Cathedral of Santiago de Compostela, the tomb of Saint James, in Santiago, Spain. The *Camino Francés* is the best-known and most-traveled of these routes. It journeys westward 800 kilometers across northern Spain, from St-Jean-Pied-de-Port at the base of the Pyrenees in France to Santiago. The *Camino Fisterra* continues ninety kilometers westward from there to the Atlantic Ocean.

Chakra: Chakras are energy centers in the body. There are seven primary chakras running from the base of the spine to the top of the head. Each chakra has a wide variety of significances and associations in such areas as theme, color, body function, physical and mental disorders, musical sounds, and elements (earth, water, etc.) to name a few. In the accompanying chart I highlight each chakra's theme and color as I refer to them in this book.

Chakra	Location	Theme	Color
7th – crown	Top of the Head	Spirituality, Enlightenment	White, Violet
6th – third eye	Center of the Forehead	Intuition, Vision, Wisdom	Purple, Indigo
5th – throat	Throat	Communication, Truth	Blue
4th – heart	Center of the Chest	Love, Compassion	Green
3rd – solar plexus	Above the Navel	Personal Power, Self-Esteem	Yellow
2nd – sacral	Below the Navel	Creativity, Sexuality, Relationships	Orange
1st – root	Base of the Spine	Will to Live, Tribal Connection	Red

A Course in Miracles (ACIM): ACIM is a spiritual thought system, a self-study curriculum designed to change the way we think about ourselves and the world we live in (see Ego). It teaches that forgiveness is the key to happiness, releasing us from guilt and bringing us healing. Although written with Christian terminology, its spiritual teachings are universal.

Ego: Ego is a thought system that believes we are our bodies, and that we are lacking in some way, imperfect in who we are, and separate from one another and from God.

Reiki: Translated as "life force energy," Reiki is an energy treatment for healing the body, mind, and spirit. The practitioner places his or her hands over the various energy centers of the body and acts as a conduit for the reception of this life force energy.

Singing Bowls: Tibetan singing bowls are metal bowls that range in size and shape. Different harmonic sounds from each bowl are created by rubbing a padded mallet around the rim, producing a continuous sound, or by striking the rim with the mallet, producing a single vibrating sound.

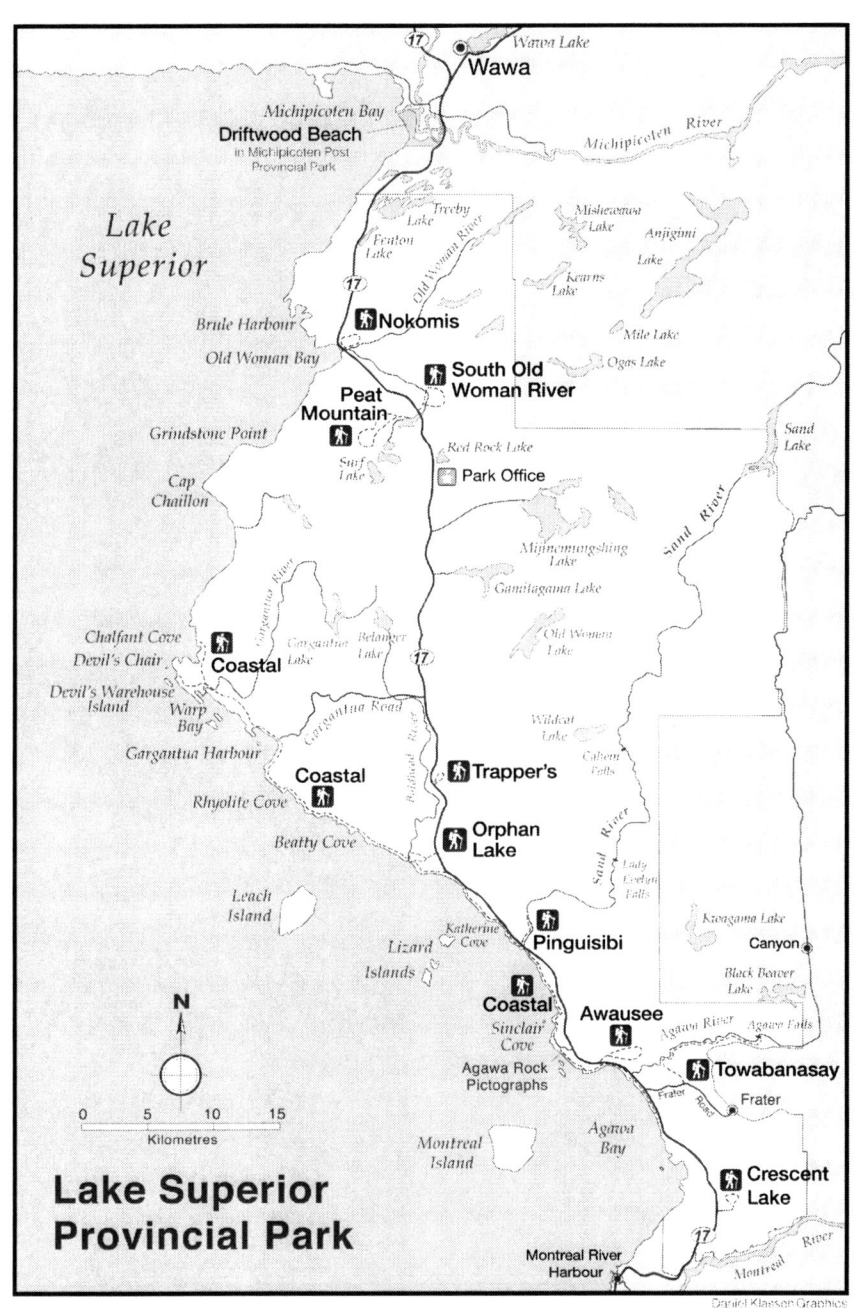

Spring 2001 — Fall 2009

Introduction

Why? Why have I been guided to write the *Led by Grace* collection? What is it about my story that you need to read? What is it about my journey that will help you live your life with serenity? And how will my story bring you any closer to knowing your Self? *Led by Grace,* written in eight parts, describes a guided process of transformation to becoming fully engaged with living *in* this world—but not being *of* this world. I have received Divine Guidance during meditations and witnessed miracles that have awakened me from my slumber of unhappiness to the Light of forgiveness. As you walk with me on my journey, you will see how this process of discovering, and living, my Self unfolded for me.

But why would you believe that I received this Divine Guidance in such a direct and vibrant manner? As with any true story, the "proof" is usually in its result. The visions I experienced in meditation made me face my life and guided me through many dark tunnels to important lessons. Ultimately, I experienced unconditional forgiveness, and with it, the miracle of living with serenity . . . most of the time. I am still very much a work-in-progress, but I have experienced great healing, joy, peace, and happiness in my life.

My journey began the moment I was born. However, for almost fifty years, I had no idea where that journey was going or—more important—that I was even *on* a journey. In the spring of 2001, my life started to change. I had my first Reiki treatment and experienced simple visions. I soon began to meditate on my own and had similar experiences. Over time, these visions, as well as miracles I experienced, grew in complexity and depth. I had no idea where this journey would take me—or the meaning of all that was happening to me—but I never found these experiences unsettling, frightening, or unsafe. Rather, I always looked forward to this time with my various guides and the journeys I took with them.

I found myself in monasteries, meadows, forests, deserts, farmhouses, rivers, and tunnels. I met my guides—a monk, an eagle, old women and men, young women and men, Inca priests, sailors, wizards, my dad, Jesus, Buddha, and God. Each vision (very often in parable form) and internal "knowing" or understanding taught me a Truth that led to my awareness and understanding that I am pure Divine Love, one with all creation.

Yet for some time, my understanding of the messages and lessons I was receiving was merely intellectual. I thought just having these experiences was enough—that I was on the path to enlightenment. But I am living a human experience; to fully engage in it, I needed to internalize the teachings, bring them into my life, and apply them to all my life experiences. This was difficult; I could not make this connection, and I did not understand that all my problems were not because of someone or something else. But the Divine is endlessly patient and non-judgmental. In the fall of 2009, I finally grasped forgiveness at the end of my forty-day, 925-kilometer pilgrimage on the Camino de Santiago de Compostela. It was the springboard for my ongoing journey to *live* with forgiveness in my life.

All of my senses were alive during my visions, and I wrote them down in great detail afterward. This, in itself, was curious; I had only ever kept a short journal in my early teens, and I had never imagined that anyone would read my journals. For years, I never reread them.

For a number of years, I was guided to write the *Led by Grace* collection, but I was unable to see past what I considered immeasurable ego concerns. Would my life not be exposed, my privacy invaded? Would others I wrote about not be affected? How could I ever deal with the overwhelming amount of material? What would my readers think?

How could I possibly do this, and how was I to present the material? It was so much easier just not to write it. Whenever I expressed my concerns to God, I was always told that everything would be all right. And that was exactly right—as it always is.

As I sat on the precipice of Cape Fisterra overlooking the Atlantic Ocean at the end of my Camino journey, God once again spoke to me about my life purpose. I was to share my message and I was now ready to do so, as described in this excerpt from the eighth and final part of *Led by Grace*.

> God says, "Write your story. Just write your story. Reread your journals and tell your story. That is what you need to do. Tell your whole story—the ups, the downs, the trouble, the pain, the joys, the realizations—tell your story."
>
> I become overwhelmed with tears as I hear God's words.
>
> God continues, "Look at the birds. They never doubt that the air will hold them up and take them where they need to go. They just know. Become like the birds and fly."
>
> I study the multitude of birds soaring, rising, and floating on the air. And then I realize that God is "pushing" me out of the nest. Tears are running down my face. I am scared of falling over the cliff. But birds leaving the nest all know how to fly. They only leave the nest when they are ready.
>
> "Feel the wind beneath your wings," God says. "You will be safe. It is time for you to leave the nest, to fly, to begin your journey. Your story is the end but also the beginning. I have nurtured you, guided you, fed you, kept you safe while you were growing until you were

ready to fly and start your life. This is where you leave the nest in the trees and fly beyond."

I am looking directly over the cliffs heading into the sea. I am emotional, I am scared . . . Then I am completely accepting, completely understanding of the truth of my readiness.

Yet it was still not until almost six months later, as I walked along Wawa Lake on my fifty-seventh birthday, that I fully understood that I needed to move forward. My journal entries were already written. I was to write my interpretation of each one and the lesson each brings into our lives. When I returned home from my walk that morning, I began to write. I wrote for several hours, and it felt good. My life purpose became an all-consuming passion.

The next day, I went hiking in Lake Superior Provincial Park. At the summit on Nokomis, I asked God if I could just have a sign that I was *really* writing *Led by Grace* as He wanted. Fifteen minutes later, I received my answer, my miracle, in the form of a lynx. He was standing on the lowest limb of a tree about six meters away from me. I had hiked that trail more than a thousand times and had never seen a lynx. The lynx and I stared at each other for a while before I headed on my way. I thanked God for this gift.

In North American native culture, lynx medicine has to do with secrets: he is the keeper of secrets, the knower of secrets. In *Medicine Cards,* Jamie Sams and David Carson write:

> To be confronted by the powerful medicine of Lynx signifies that you do not know something about yourself or others . . . Brother or Sister Lynx can teach you of your personal power and of things you have forgotten about yourself. (Sams and Carson, 1999, 109-110)

I received a sign that I should continue to write in this way, but there was still much I was to learn about myself in the process. Writing *Led by Grace* became a paradox. The more I worked through my journal entries—rereading them, meditating on them, and interpreting them—the harder it was to publish. Each time I revisited my entire journey, I grew to a greater understanding and awareness of the layers within each entry. Each time I thought I was finished, I would reread the beginning and grasp so much more depth, richness, and wisdom in each experience. Each meditation is still as vivid as when I experienced it. This cycle continued three times until I realized that I just needed to publish my understanding at this time.

Led by Grace is exactly as I received it, in the order that I received it, and with my reactions and emotions—anger, rage, guilt, joys, bliss, peace—that I experienced along the way. It begins with my first visions in 2001 and ends with my pilgrimage on the Camino de Santiago de Compostela eight years later—the end of the collection but not the end of my journey. *In the Beginning* is the first book in the collection.

All of our paths will be different, but Truth is found in all of them. I am a messenger of these Truths and an example of how they lead to true happiness, love, peace, and joy. *Led by Grace* is for you—to place yourself in each journal entry, to reflect on the interpretations I provide, and to apply each lesson to your life. I pray that you find something in this collection that helps guide you to your Self.

In the Beginning

Spring 2001—Spring 2002

My First Steps

SPRING 2001

I have my first Reiki treatment in early April, and experience my first vision of colors. During each subsequent treatment, I have these same spontaneous experiences, and soon begin to meditate on my own at home and while hiking. I am introduced to settings, a guide, and themes that weave themselves throughout my ongoing visions. I become witness to my first miracles when aspects of my visions materialize in the outside world.

> I see each of the colors of the rainbow alternating across the screen of my vision. Then I am in a bathtub and see and feel all the colors as they float down and envelop me. When I am bathed in red, I stand up, look in the mirror, and see the red of my blood flowing through my arteries.
>
> . . .

I am in a monastery made mostly of marble. It is white and open-aired, and it has huge colonial pillars both inside and out. I am in the middle of a large group of monks. I dare to open my eyes and look around. Close by, a female monk looks directly at me and is extremely sad. When I look around the large room, a male monk among the pillars is wildly waving his arms, smiling, and welcoming me.

...

I am in the monastery again, and one of the monks comes to me. He is my guide. I cannot see his face, but he is rather short and wearing white. We walk from the monastery on to the surrounding grounds. The gardens around the monastery are beautiful, with very low-lying groundcover of primarily small white flowers. We walk to an ornately carved stone bench at the edge of a cliff. It is a breathtaking view with a mountain range across the valley. Then I am following my guide along the narrow trail back to the monastery.

"Why is the path only wide enough for one?" I ask.

"You need to be led. You are not ready to go beside me yet," he replies.

Back at the monastery, I hear the monks chanting. I try to relax by focusing on my left eye, and then tell myself to relax the eye. I then hear my monk, and he starts to lead me. He tells me to do the same with my left ear, and I am easily able to do it. I have trouble isolating my right eye and right ear but finally can feel them. He tells me when I am starting to focus sufficiently. We go through isolating my lips, cheeks, tongue, hands, shoulders, elbows, and feet. I suggest I try to isolate my heart, but I cannot feel it. Then my guide suggests

I hold my heart. I take it out and hold it in my hands as it beats loudly.

"See what a good heart you have," he says.

I cry.

. . .

I am with my monk guide on a long staircase in the middle of my brain. It is quite noisy—almost like the hold of a ship. My body feels tingly.

"Where are the lesions from my seizure?" I ask.

We go up to the spot and see just a small lesion remaining.

"Where did one of my relatives have his stroke?"

We go over and see a gaping wound.

"Where was the source of another relative's aneurysm?"

We walk down the stairs to the "basement" and see the leak.

We come back up to where we were. I can see a window overhead, but the ladder does not reach high enough to get to it.

"How do I get out?" I ask.

"Over time, the gap between the ladder and the window closes. You've already walked a few steps," my monk answers as a warm bright light shines through the window.

. . .

I see a beautiful flower, yellow in the center and pinkish red on the outside with long stamens, but I can only see it on exhalation. The flower image starts in the center of my vision, and then moves up and around in a clockwise circle to the bottom.

On my way home from hiking Nokomis, I borrow plant books to try to find the flower, but nothing resembles it. Two weeks later, I am hiking Peat Mountain, and shortly after starting out, my eye is drawn to a flower. It is the exact flower from my meditation! There are hundreds and hundreds of these flowers the entire length of the trail. I am awestruck. I pick one to bring home and identify from a reference book. But even with the flower in hand, nothing resembles it in any of the books I borrow. Finally, I decide to call a botanist. He immediately identifies it as the trout lily or alder tongue.

...

I cross over a bridge into a meadow. Children in long dresses and hats are playing. There is a farmhouse in the distance. When I walk through the fields, the grass springs up behind me so that my trail disappears.

Three days later, I am looking through a magazine and see a picture of this exact meadow with the children playing and a farmhouse in the distance. I am filled with awe.

My Interpretation

I have opened the door to the world of my Self and taken my first steps inside. My first vision is with the colors of the seven chakras. At this time, I am not even aware of chakras. I bask in each color, but when I am enveloped in red, I stand up and observe my body. Red is the color of the root chakra—the chakra energy that resonates with our will to live and our connection to the group beliefs of family and community.

The monastery becomes my spiritual "home," that place I return to time and again to be grounded by its serenity. The meadow with the children and the farmhouse also will continue to be the backdrop for many of my meditations and the location for great healing to come.

What I already know of my inner turmoil and my outward presentation appears as the sad girl and the exuberant male. I was leading what seemed like a charmed life—I had success, fame, wealth, health, and four wonderful children. I was married to a good man and good father. People always said that I was born under a lucky star—and they were right. My life flowed easily. I always was in the right place at the right time, and I succeeded at pretty much anything I did. Perfect opportunities and jobs always just appeared. But as time marched on, my outside world became increasingly divergent from my inside world. Externally, all was going well, but I felt completely empty inside. Feeling good became more fleeting. I did not really know what I was feeling, and I could not verbalize my anger.

I learn to focus on isolating and then letting go of various body parts. Feeling my ears, lips, eyes, feet, and so on becomes relatively easy as the meditation continues, but when I take over and try to feel my heart, I cannot. I still need to be led; I am not ready. Only when my guide leads me can I feel my heart. This theme of having a good heart—of holding my wonderful heart in my hands—will come up many times. But it is so difficult for me to hear this. Even in the meditation, tears flow. I do not believe I have a good heart; I am not good. My monk tells me that I *am* good, but this is beyond me. I will continue to be told this: I need to love myself and know that I am good.

For years, I would cry as I related my visions to two of my friends. The tears were never tears of sadness; they were tears of being overwhelmed by my experiences. Even now, when I get that sense of weepiness, I know that it means I am close to the Divine within.

In February 1993, I had a nocturnal grand mal seizure, followed by a second one two months later on Good Friday (the symbolic date of the death of the ego). I thought that my life had come to an end. I saw the seizures as a weakness and was embarrassed about them. I remember a family relation telling me I needed to listen to my body. Inwardly, I was so annoyed that they would suggest that I had anything to do with my seizures, this weakness! It took me years to realize the truth of what I had been told. Our bodies are a mirror of our emotional, mental, and spiritual well-being. I had imploded. I had completely shut down to the world. I was denying my life. My emotions needed to be released, noticed, given love to heal.

I am shown the physical signs of my seizures and the brain trauma in two relatives. But then I see a bright, warm light beyond this place of the body, this place of noise, confinement, and disease. I cannot yet reach it because the gap is too great. This gap closes when we take steps, when we walk with the guidance of our Higher Self.

I experience two manifestations early in my journey. With the synchronicity of seeing my flower on my hike and the exact picture of my meadow visualization, I am given evidence that I am not making this all up. I never doubt when I experience a vision or write about it afterwards, yet after the fact, I continually question whether this is all just my imagination, a fabrication. It will be many years before I truly let go of any doubt that I am receiving guidance from God.

How Do We Bring This into Our Lives?

We all have different experiences in meditation. I was fortunate to have had spontaneous visions during my first Reiki treatments, which I was able to repeat during my own meditations. More often, however, the process of reaching that place of focused attention seems more daunting. Endless lists, concerns, and distractions keep our minds busy and unfocused. There are numerous ways of maintaining focus—concentrating on breathing, gazing softly at a candle or light, chanting, focusing on individual parts of the body—while being in an environment conducive to relaxation, be that a designated area in our house or out in nature.

Wherever and however we meditate, we need to be gentle with ourselves. The harder we try to see colors and auras, experience inner peace and serenity, or hear messages, the more likely we will end up feeling disappointed, self-judgmental, and frustrated, and believing that these experiences are just not ours to have because we not spiritual enough or good enough. We need to let go of our ego expectations of what is *supposed* to happen. Nothing is *supposed* to happen. What will happen is exactly what we need at the time. Judging ourselves as ready enough or well-read enough or knowledgeable enough only leads to self-criticism and doubt. We need to relax and let be. If our minds race around with a million thoughts, we need to acknowledge that and say, "Not now, thank you. I am staying open and relaxed with no expectations." Experiencing a clear, thoughtless mind is indeed a gift.

We need to explore the "unusual" things that happen so frequently. We need to go beyond just *noticing* the "coincidences" to *exploring* their meaning. The reasons behind them may not always be apparent at the time, but at some point, they will. Experiencing these signs helps deepen the belief that we are more than just a body.

Crossing My Bridges

∞

June 14, 2001

Yesterday, I was hiking toward an old fort on the banks of the Michipicoten River. I heard voices that sounded like boys and girls partying. I wondered why they were out of school. My dog, Nicky, did not seem to react at all. After a while, I wondered if those children were happy or in trouble. When I got to the fort, there was no one there.

About a month ago, I talked to a friend about issues I was having in my marriage. This was the first time I had ever verbalized my feelings. While it was a relief to finally give my emotions a concrete voice, it brought up the reality of how my marriage problems would affect the children. This plays a role during my Reiki treatment this morning.

> I am going down a black passage. My guide tells me
> I don't need to hang on to the side, just walk. I start
> to walk.
>   "Now try to run," I hear.

"How can I run in the pitch black?" I ask. I try, and it gradually gets brighter until I am in the bright sunlight. "Does it ever get cloudy?" I ask.

"Yes, but total sun or clouds," he responds.

We are then in a crowded outdoor flea market with cobblestone roads. People are jostling all around us. Since I want to be somewhere quieter, we get to a field by ourselves. I see my children walking toward us over a small grassy hill. I introduce them, and one asks my guide, "Are you helping my mom?"

"Yes. Are you?"

"I'm getting better at it," they reply.

Then my children say good-bye and walk back to where they came from. I am very emotional.

I start to cry in the meditation and on the table.

My guide tells me the children will all be all right. He takes my hand.

"Why did you do that?" I ask. He has never touched me before.

"Because you need to be touched, to feel my energy."

I can feel the energy through my hand, elbow, and up to my shoulder, but I cannot feel it in the rest of my body. I calm down.

We start climbing and arrive at the pinnacle of a mountain, just big enough for the both of us to stand on. There is a beautiful view in the distance, but there is a big cavern directly in front of us. He tells me not to look down. Across the way, I notice that there are colors. My guide says for me to imagine them. I tell him that I now know the colors and what they mean.

"So spin around and see what you see."

I see blue first. I lie down, and blue "snowflakes" fall from the sky and envelop me. Then yellow, orange, and finally, red. When I am completely covered in red, I raise my hand. As before, I stand up and look in a mirror. I see all of my arteries and my heart, and I am totally red with blood inside. Then I am enveloped in purple and finally, white, where it is particularly calm. I don't want to leave. When I stand up, I am wearing a white robe—just as my guide is. I take his hand, and this time, I have no trouble feeling his energy move through my entire torso and then into my head.

I ask, "How do we get down?" I then suggest sliding down, as it would be fun.

"You don't want to go down. Why don't we take a bridge?"

I look around and can't see any bridge, just the valley below.

He steps from our pinnacle to a golden bridge, which is visible for about a meter ahead and behind him—just enough distance for me to follow. As we walk along the bridge, only a short distance ahead and behind us is visible.

We are headed toward the monastery when he asks if I want to go somewhere else.

"How?" I ask.

"Take another bridge."

We turn left, and another bridge becomes visible wherever we step. We arrive at a community. Children are laughing and playing, throwing a ball.

"Can they see me or know I'm here?" I ask.

"Yes."

We walk through town filled with horse-drawn carriages. One man tips his hat and smiles.

"Why did he do that?"

"Because he wanted you to know," he says, but he doesn't explain further.

"Who are they?"

"They are all dead and have chosen to come back at this time, place, and age," he explains.

We go back to the bridge.

"How did you know where the bridge was?"

"There are many bridges."

When we return to the intersection where we'd changed bridges, I see numerous bridges going in different directions, like spokes on a wheel. I had not seen this initially because my back was to the intersection.

We arrive at the monastery and see the sunset.

"Take a sunbeam and feel its warmth," he says.

A sunbeam goes through my head and down my body. It circles my organs, my heart in particular.

"Take out your heart and massage it and kiss it. Your heart is good."

I do, touching it tenderly, and then I put it back, attaching the arteries and veins with snaps like a knapsack.

Then the music gets very loud, calling us to the monastery. Again I am in the middle among many. I see the girl, and she smiles. The man at the edge waves and smiles.

My Interpretation

This is the first appearance of dark tunnels as the starting point in my meditations. They play a large role in many of my future meditations. Making my way through a tunnel is a metaphor for moving from the fear-based ego to the love-based True Self. I do not need to hold on or be fearful—I can simply walk or run once I understand that I will be safe.

In the Beginning

I am told that what we look at is either totally light (the Divine) or covered with clouds (the ego). Belief in the ego, the belief in separation, only obscures the Divine. The Divine does not go away or change. It just waits for the clouds to pass. Belief in Oneness is complete: you cannot believe in both the ego (that you are your body) and your Divine Self. There cannot be partial clouds.

Every mother has an innate instinct to protect her children and is concerned for their well-being. My four children enter my meditations for the first time, and my overwhelming emotions pour out through my tears while having my treatment. As I will be told time and time again, they will be all right. The conversation between the monk and the children is about helping me. It is my very first lesson in learning to receive love, here in the form of help.

Colors become a vehicle for me to distinguish physical sensations. When I am enveloped in the white robe—the white of the crown chakra—I am able to fully absorb the clear, joyful energy of my guide for the first time. The lessons of the colors will eventually allow me to connect them with the different chakras, sense which color or chakra feels peaceful, and understand why either discomfort or bliss manifests in specific ones. But I am only in the early stage now.

I am introduced to the existence of bridges that span the vast valley below to the mountain range on the other side. Because of them, we do not have to go down to the valley, back to one's life as a separate self, an ego self, only to repeat the climb up the other side. This route is such a long way and ripe with all the trappings of the ego. There are still challenges and lessons on the other side, but the bridges allow us to get to the place of those spiritual challenges and not spend all of our lives searching and wallowing in the valley below, perhaps not even seeing the light because the mountains are shading it.

How Do We Bring This into Our Lives?

We need to believe and know there are bridges that allow us to make our way more easily to where we need to go—and we need to step onto them. A bridge may appear as a trusted friend's guidance, our spiritual path and teachings, a book we have read, or a speech we have heard that resonates with us. It is something that, if we "step" onto it, will allow us to bypass the long journey and take us to our destination for learning.

The bridges are visible only when we step on them, and then only for a meter ahead and behind, about the span of our aura. We are drawn toward the "aura of our bridges," and then we become part of that aura. Some people, places, and things we gravitate to, as they are full of life, while others make us uncomfortable just being in their presence. We need to use intuition to help guide us to our bridges.

The Body's Flaws, The Spirit's Perfection

∞

June 26, 2001

My meditation begins before my Reiki Master comes into the room.

> I am picking flowers; when she puts her hands on my head, I feel a power say, "Go on."
> "But it is so nice here just to pick flowers."
> "But you can't grow if you do not move forward."
> I reluctantly move, and my guide appears.
> "I didn't see you come," I say.
> "I am always here."
> We come upon a small, beautifully maintained graveyard. He says that important people are buried here, but there are no names on the simple crosses. "Everyone is important," he says.

We climb up a mountain and come to the monastery and sit on the stone bench.

"It is so beautiful up here," I say.

"What makes it beautiful?"

"There are no flaws. Nature is perfect."

"Look at that tree." The tree has a large split around one of its branches. "See, that tree is flawed, but a branch grew up around it and made it strong. Now look at the crabgrass. It grows among the grass, but the grass survives. But if the cut is too big or the crabgrass too plentiful, then the tree and the grass will die. Nature is not without physical flaws, but it adapts to make itself strong."

I draw a moonbeam through my head into my body. I feel the heat down to my groin, but it will not enter my legs. I go through the colors—green, where I can smell the grass and the grapes, blue, yellow, and then red, where I feel agitated. When I go to purple, I feel calm.

I want to go for a walk on the bridges.

"You lead the way," he says.

"But I can't see them."

"Close your eyes, and you'll see them."

I do see them. "But if I open my eyes, I can't see them," I say.

"I'll lead you to the edge, and you take a step."

There is a myriad of bridges going in all directions.

"I'm afraid I may mistake something as a bridge and fall," I say.

"I won't let you get hurt."

With that new confidence, I head out. I am on a bridge with a very small railing. My guide follows, and we arrive at a field with lots of children playing.

"This is for the children," he says.

But I want to go somewhere for adults. We go across another bridge and arrive at a cliff. I start to climb but am soon frozen. I have the feeling of falling backward. He says to keep going. I feel sick and scared to death. I am breathing fast, but I continue to climb. At the top, there is a large overhang. I don't know how I am going to make it up. But then my guide is at the top, and he reaches down and pulls me up by the arm as my body dangles.

"You are safe now," he says.

I lie on the ground, trying to calm down and catch my breath.

"You can get up now," he says.

When I stand up and look around, I see a huge, light blue dome. I find myself inside, and it is incredible. It feels so wonderful and peaceful, like heaven perhaps.

I say, "I don't want to leave."

He says, "But there are no people here."

I reluctantly leave and wonder how I am going to get down the cliff.

He says, "Just take this other path down."

"Why didn't I just take this easy route up?"

"Because there is a one-way gate at the bottom. You can get out, but you can't get in."

We walk along the bridge back to the monastery. All of the monks are wearing black this time instead of the white robes I usually see them in. Sparks from all of them fly toward me. It is their love.

I ask my guide, "What is love?"

"Physical and emotional caring for people," he replies.

Led by Grace

My Interpretation

In the beginning of this meditation, I am so peaceful. I do not want to leave. Why do I need to? This identifies a potential trap that we may fall into on the quest for enlightenment. We meditate, connect with our Higher Self, see auras—even levitate and bend spoons—and we think we have become truly spiritual. But have we learned to live our human lives? Have we dealt with the issues that plague us? The incredible attraction to discovering our spirituality typically begins in the higher chakras. To open these chakras is essential, but without opening the lower three chakras—the chakras of our relationships and self-esteem—we cannot *live* a truly spiritual life. We will constantly be pulled out of our sense of peace through any number of triggers (something we react to because of past experiences).

The view from the bench at the monastery is indeed very beautiful. My guide asks me what makes it beautiful. I do not respond that the sunrise and sunsets are spectacular in their colors; I do not say that the rugged mountain peaks beyond are magical; I do not say the vista itself is breathtaking. I say that there are no flaws; I say that nature is perfect. It is with the eyes of my Higher Self that all I look upon is perfect. I only associate this perfection with nature; however, *everything* is perfect—and everything includes us. My guide uses my belief in nature's perfection to illustrate the connection between our Divine Perfection and our bodies. He points out the cut in the tree and the crabgrass overtaking the grass. Every one of us has suffered "cuts" or trauma in some form and to some degree, and every one of us has experienced "crabgrass" or pressure, whether self-inflicted or inflicted by others. He teaches that we are able to thrive despite these flaws. We are not flawless as humans, but our Souls are perfection. It is in working through the colors of the chakras that I am being led to first notice my "cuts" and to react to them so I can heal them.

I am shown how to see the bridges with my third eye and to learn to trust in their presence. A bridge leads to a children's meadow. I am to learn something here, but I choose not to; I bypass that lesson. This leads to experiencing my first actual fear in meditation—the fear of falling, of hurting myself. In many future meditations, this same fear returns. But my guide is there to help me, and once over this fear, I experience a peace that is so wonderful that I imagine it is what heaven must be like. Once again, I am told that I cannot stay here, as I am living a human experience and need to return to my life to learn to live with this peace while in a body. Sometimes the journey to this peaceful place can be difficult, but once we have experienced this connectedness, the route back to our body, our earthly life, is "direct" and easier.

When we return to the monastery, the monks are wearing black rather than their previous white robes. Any preconceived association of good and evil symbolism is squelched when love explodes from the monks. Love is the physical, emotional caring and compassion for all people.

How Do We Bring This into Our Lives?

We are not perfect as humans. To think that we must be so simply closes the door to compassion and happiness for ourselves—and to our compassion and wishes for happiness for others. How we heal from what has happened in the past or what is happening in the present determines our happiness. We can believe that our traumas "define" us and, therefore, simply survive; on the other hand, we can understand Divine Perfection in ourselves and others and heal our wounds and thrive despite them.

On our route to awareness, we often face significant obstacles. Returning to our Self is simple in principle. It requires nothing more than changing our minds about Who we are, but practically, the tenaciousness of the ego makes the journey difficult and fraught with challenges, for we do not give up who we *think* we are easily. Our resistance creates the hurdles and barriers we face, but ultimately, we will all know our Divine Essence—when we are alive or at our passing.

A Pot of Gold

∞

SEPTEMBER 14, 2001

This is the first time in months I have been able to meditate at all. At the first lookout on Nokomis, I concentrate on my breathing and eventually keep focused.

> Everything is black. I start walking and arrive at the meadow. I see a band immediately to my left, but they aren't marching. I wonder if they are playing America's national anthem after the 9/11 tragedy, but I can't make out the tune. A short while later, I see a horse on the right with no rider.
>
> My monk guide appears from behind, and we go to the monastery. It is very sunny. Even though I can't make out faces, I feel that I recognize many of the monks. My guide and I go sit on the stone bench, and I ask if we can go through the colors. I feel and see them all, but I don't

notice any significant change in feeling. I open my eyes and see a beautiful rainbow.

"Rainbows are the harmony of all emotions in a truly peaceful and perfect way. The pot of gold at the end is no illusion. The healthy blend of emotions is worth more than anything—even a pot of gold. A rainbow comes after a storm's dark clouds, lightning, thunder, and turmoil. After you've come out, you want a rainbow. You've been living in the eye of a tornado—relatively peaceful at the center but impossible to get out of calmly. Now you have a means to get out of that tornado," he says.

"What should I do?"

"Your answer will come to you."

We go to the monastery, and I feel the power of all the other monks. I walk back to the meadow and turn around, with a tear in my eye, to see my guide waving good-bye.

My Interpretation

We all marvel at the beauty of a rainbow, that perfect blend of fused colors arching through the sky. The colors of the rainbow are the exact colors, in order, of the seven chakras. It is said that where the rainbow touches the earth is a pot of gold, symbolically that which is most valuable. My guide distinguishes the "worth" of a pot of gold brimming with materialism from the far more valuable pot of gold embracing our healthy blend of emotions. When we are balanced and open in all of our chakras, we *are* a "pot of gold," a most precious and valuable gift for ourselves, and for others.

I go through the chakra colors with my guide and, for the first time, do not feel a difference in them; I feel peaceful in this place. Energy freely moves through my upper and lower chakras. I am shown what the pot of gold *feels* like.

Even though my life appears to be calm, smooth, and easy from the outside, I am living within a tornado, a volatile force with the potential to wipe out anything in its path, and it is holding me prisoner. I know I am unhappy but cannot really explain it. I do not see that I am in a tornado. How do I get out of it? I am not told specifically—only that I will know. I need to go through the many lessons to safely internalize my ultimate forgiveness.

How Do We Bring This into Our Lives?

I have not taken the time to meditate over the summer months—partly because I am not comfortable with telling people that I meditate but also because I have not had much alone time. Yet a meditation practice is a commitment to be with our Self on a regular basis. It is through such a commitment that our experience deepens over time.

After a personal storm, regardless of the form that storm takes, there is always the possibility of a rainbow—a healing, a blending and balancing of our emotional, physical, mental, and spiritual bodies. But unless we *look* for that rainbow, we will only see the aftermath of a storm, the destruction it has created. There is *always* a light at the end, always a light that creates a rainbow. We need to focus on what we look for when our storm ends; if it does not seem to end, we need to start to walk out of it. The pot of gold is serenity, peace, and happiness, which are truly most valuable for us; with them, blessings come in so many other ways.

As with many things in life, the process of self-discovery is exactly that—a process that needs to evolve as understanding and awareness grow. We may not know the final destination, but we will be guided to, and know, our next markers along the way. For each of us, this process will vary in time—but not in purpose. We need to be aware of this process so that we see each lesson as the growth that it is.

Reflections

∞

September 17, 2001

It is a nice day for hiking. I have stopped at a lookout on Nokomis to meditate.

> Although I am in darkness, I am able to walk down the path quickly. Since I don't want to leave this darkness, I picture myself inside a cave. When I make myself go outside, my guide appears.
> "Do you want to go to the bridges?" he asks.
> "Can you just show me where the bridge starts?"
> "Try to find it yourself," he says.
> I look around the grassy edge of the cliff for signs. I see an indentation in the grass and assume that it is where people have stepped off the cliff. I gingerly put my foot over the edge, and the bridge appears.

I lead as my guide and I walk along the bridge and take the first right onto another. It ends at a huge cliff. I see a way that looks easier than climbing up, and I start walking around it. I come upon a big gap that I try to get across, but I cannot. *So much for the easy way*, I think.

I go back and start to climb the cliff using handholds and footholds. But I fall and badly hurt my arm. I am so surprised that my guide let me hurt myself. I thought he would have caught me—he has told me he would protect me. I try again and make it to the top.

I see huge gems arranged in a circular pattern with a diamond in the center. The gems reflect light and make a pattern, but the pattern is not connected—light spreads out in individual beams. I walk around to the other side and see that the reflection from this view is completely different. The pattern is beautiful, colorful, and connected so that the light becomes fused.

My guide and I go back on the bridges to the monastery and sit on the bench. I again look at the view and notice, in a small part of the landscape, the same beautiful reflection of connected light rays that I had seen from the gems. My guide tells me that it has always been there, I just hadn't seen it.

I ask him if the bridges always lead to the same place. He says yes, but that there are many more bridges I haven't even seen yet.

My Interpretation

I am now being taught to take steps by myself, although I know that my guide is always with me. I am being guided, not led. I need to discover how to move forward, first by locating the bridges and then by determining which ones to follow. I take clues left behind by others—a worn pathway that has been used many times before. Others who have gone before us can help guide us. All bridges lead to the same place—our Divine Self—but it may take walking on many of them before we arrive at this awareness of our True Essence.

I try to take the easy way but to no avail. I must climb the cliff I am taken to. I am so surprised that I am "allowed" to fall, that I feel such pain. But I try again and make my way to the top. Sometimes the obstacles we face will seem daunting, and perhaps painful, but they are the route that will get us to our lesson for our growth.

I see precious gemstones (us) circling a diamond (God), symbolizing our connection to God. From my initial vantage point, the gems are reflecting unconnected, colored patterns of light outward like a star, mirroring the belief that we are all separate. By moving around to the opposite side, I see a completely different image: a continuous light fused into a beautiful blend of color, mirroring our connection to each other. I see the Oneness of us all. I see with different eyes; I see with vision rather than with sight.

How Do We Bring This into Our Lives?

Even with a bridge, there is often no easy route in this classroom of Self-awareness and personal growth. The easy way, the shortcuts we try to take, will often take us to a roadblock. For on our journey, we may need to learn lessons that may be difficult and cause temporary pain. But we will move through this short-term pain when we are connected with our Higher Self. We just need to be willing to step forward to our ultimate healing.

We need to be willing to see ourselves and others with different eyes—with the eyes of vision. Which view *feels* better? Which of our long-time beliefs, expectations, and patterns are in line with this vision? Vision allows us to see beyond what we find difficult in the behavior or beliefs of others to the Divine in them. When we can see our Divine Oneness, we free ourselves from anxiety, "unforgiveness," and fear.

What Looks Easy Is Not Always So

∞

SEPTEMBER 25, 2001

I am meditating at home.

>I go through a dark passage.
>"I know the way now. I don't have to hold out my hands," I say. In no time, I walk into a wall. The passage goes around many corners and down some stairs.
>"Your hands guide you through," my guide says.
>I make my way through to the light. I am on a baseball diamond, and my daughter is playing.
>My son walks up to me. "You need to be happy, Mom. I love you," he says.
>My daughter can't understand what is going on.
>My son tells her that I need to know they love me.
>"Mom, aren't you happy?" she asks.

"Sometimes—but not all of the time."

My guide comes along, and the two of us walk toward the monastery. However, rather than going across a bridge, I want to walk around. It is a beautiful field, and the cliff to the monastery is just to our right. We don't talk; we just enjoy the wonderful, peaceful feeling.

We come upon a small river. I think it will be easy to cross by just stepping across on some boulders. But as I get closer, the boulders seem to disappear. I think the water looks shallow, and I can just walk across. I still have a long way to go and don't want my pants, shoes, and socks to get wet. I take them off but leave my other clothes on. As I start across, the river gets progressively deeper until it is well over my head, and all my clothes get wet. I am tired and chilled from my swim upstream.

My guide is there on the other side, helping me out and drying me off with a large towel. "Sometimes the path seems easy at first, but as you continue along, it may become difficult," he says.

I am soon warmed up, and my clothes dry quickly in the sun. He gives me a hug.

My Interpretation

Now that I have been through dark tunnels, I think that all of them will be the same and be easy for me to navigate. Since they represent our walk through the ego to our Higher Self, they will be neither. The ego will try to block our way, frighten us, and make the way difficult. We need to have confidence that we will get through.

For the second time (see "Crossing My Bridges"), two of my children appear and take the role of teachers and parents, telling me of their love.

Rather than take a bridge, I elect to walk around to the monastery. I have chosen to ignore my direct route because where I am feels so peaceful. I am still walking on my journey, but I delay; until I am with my Self, any sense of peace is temporary.

I encounter a seemingly small obstacle—a river I believe can be easily crossed. I do not become completely naked, I do not fully commit to it, and I am not prepared for it. As I enter the river, the journey becomes very difficult. The challenging—and unexpected—swim upstream stretches my physical and emotional capabilities, and my clothes still get wet. In a future meditation in this book (see "Getting Naked, Experiencing Love"), I cross this same river fully naked and have a completely different experience.

My guide is waiting for me on the other side to warm me physically with a towel and emotionally with a hug. He teaches me that, as we walk along our journey to our Self, what starts out seeming easy sometimes becomes difficult. He is foretelling the story of my journey. I am currently beginning on a road that is "easy." I have wonderful visions and feel connected to "something." As my journey continues—and I look at what triggers me, what blocks me from my Self—the road is not as easy. My river becomes deeper, and I am tired, but I am always warmed and loved on the other side. My experience is typical; the specifics may differ for each reader, but the pattern is likely common.

How Do We Bring This into Our Lives?

As we move along our path to our Higher Self, we will face challenges because our beliefs and behavior as separate selves are so ingrained. Some may be painful or frightening, but we need to know that we *will* make it to through them and we *will* be helped and taken care of. The key is to take a step through the darkness, climb what seems to be a mountain, cross a river that threatens to sweep us away.

When we initially move along the journey to Self, the way can appear easy and straightforward. But as we continue to walk and look upon the roots of our triggers, what our blocks are, the path may become difficult; one uncovered block may lead to another and yet another. Sometimes we may feel as though we "can't take anymore." But when we are taking this journey with the awareness that we are not traveling it alone, we realize that we *can* do it, that we *need* to continue, and that we *will* always be met with warmth and love.

So often, we only seek guidance, pray, or ask for help from God (or our name for "All That Is") when we are in turmoil. When things are going well around us, nothing is going wrong, and we feel we have everything under control, we have the tendency to stay in this seeming peace, not realizing or thinking that we still need to move forward to awareness of our True Self. We will still face obstacles; little obstacles may become increasingly difficult and take us "over our head." Our journey to our Self is ongoing. We are wise to take the bridges that are presented to us.

A Stranger

∞

OCTOBER 3, 2001

My friend has just returned from Toronto and brought me a CD of singing bowls. We decide to try to meditate together. Before doing so, I read her my recent meditations.

> I relax quickly although I find myself drifting to the children's activities. Although my Reiki Master is not here, I feel her presence and her hands on my head. It feels very warm.
>
> My guide comes right away. I am surprised that I didn't have to walk through the dark tunnel.
>
> "You did your preparation by talking to your friend about your meditations," he explains.
>
> We walk to the edge of the meadow overlooking the valley. There is a lone tree to the right of us.

He says, "Don't try to find where the bridges are. Just put your feet over the edge."

I sit down and stretch my legs down over the edge. Finally, I see and feel the bridge as my foot rests on it. I carefully lower myself down, quite afraid of falling. I help my guide down, even though he doesn't look like he needs a hand!

It is beautiful and sunny. We walk along the bridge; I stop to admire the view and look down. There is a city below—everything is in miniature.

When we reach the other side, we walk through a hole in the cliff wall. I hope there are no bats. We come upon a ladder that leads up to a manhole cover. We climb up and lift the cover into the meadow where children are playing. However, this time the children notice me and start jumping on me. We are all rolling around on the ground except for one boy who stands apart.

"I'm not supposed to play with big people," he says.

I kneel down and say, "Now am I big?"

He comes over and gives me a big hug.

"You are a good hugger," I say.

"That's what my mom always used to say," he replies.

"Where's your mom?" I ask.

"She's not here." He shows me a picture of her. I don't recognize her. He says, "If you see my mom, tell her how much I love her and how much I miss her."

I guess that this is heaven for children.

My guide and I climb back down the manhole, but I find a different tunnel back to the cliff wall and onto a different bridge. This time, the weather is cold, rainy, and windy. I have to lie down on the bridge and edge myself forward since the bridge is swinging wildly. My guide says we need to take a different path. We turn onto another bridge into the sun.

When we arrive at the monastery, I enter alone. I feel wonderful. I meet my guide again and we go to the bench, where I see my colors. First yellow, but very shortly after, red flashes. I feel a tremendous change in my body. My stomach is in knots; I am tense. "Get me out of red!" I yell.

I go to purple, and the change is dramatic. I think that white will be even better. And it is! I go outside my body and see myself sitting on the bench. I take the time to look around. I see meadows all around the monastery and huge cliffs with a large hole. I see people on the bridges, but because the bridges only illuminate where you stand on them, they look like hundreds of fireflies. I see my friend I am meditating with in a field knee-deep in dandelions with fluff blowing in the wind. I try being in red once more, but the negative body feelings return. I quickly go back to white and find myself in a warm cloud.

I come back to my body. My guide and I are sitting quietly on the bench when a stranger comes up and asks if he can sit there too. I am in the middle, and it is not nearly as uncomfortable as I would have thought. He and my guide talk briefly in a foreign language. We all hold hands, and it is beautiful and warm.

The stranger says good-bye and leaves. My guide and I sit for a while longer. When I see my friend leaving the field, I know it is time to end the meditation.

My Interpretation

I am now guided to find the bridges without looking for clues, without needing logic before taking a step—without needing to figure it all out beforehand. I need to trust that there will always be a bridge that is perfect for my journey.

The bridge to the meadow is tranquil and beautiful, but I still must pass through a tunnel and climb a ladder. The bridges will shorten our journey, but they may still often present challenges once across.

In a previous meditation (see "Crossing My Bridges"), I arrived at a children's meadow but did not want to stay there. I am presented with this scenario once more because there is something for me to learn or hear. Today, it seems that I am to pass on a message to a young boy's mother that he loves her and misses her. This is the first time I have been given this type of message to relay.

When I leave the meadow, I take a different tunnel back and end up on a bridge that is very scary and unpleasant. This bridge is not for me, and my guide tells me that I need to get to a different bridge. Some frightening bridges are meant for me, but this is not one of them.

I experience strong physical sensations today when I am "with" the different chakra colors. I am very agitated in red, the color of the root chakra, the energy of group association and beliefs of our family and society. I am not balanced in this chakra. When I am with white, the color of the crown chakra, I feel such peace and calm. When I am there, I am able to leave my body, become a true observer, and see with clear vision. I see the monastery surrounded by meadows; both places hold great meaning for me.

From this place of separation from my body, I can see hundreds of bridges as people walk on them. They have the appearance of fireflies, those magical creations that draw our eyes to them. Their light glows for all to see. We are as fireflies—our Inner Light is always on, but we do not always see it. Yet it is easily visible when we walk on our bridge toward awareness.

A stranger comes and asks if he can join us on the stone bench. I will find out who he is, in time. It is tight on the bench but not uncomfortable—my anticipation of discomfort does not materialize. Adding another guide is not uncomfortable; it is warm. My guide and the stranger speak in a language I do not understand, that I am not yet able to comprehend. It is the language of Divine Love.

How Do We Bring This into Our Lives?

Most of us make decisions with logic, with some analysis of the various possible outcomes based on historical evidence and our comfort level with risk. We need to move toward making decisions based on our Inner Knowing of which bridge, which direction, will take us where we *are* to go, not where we *think* we should go. We need to take a step based on this awareness, and there will be a bridge.

When we cross our bridge, what is on the other side is meant for us in some way. If we decide not to stay, we will be taken back there again and again, until we see or hear something for our growth. We may not grasp this at the time. In fact, we may often not "get it," but eventually, when we least expect it, we will understand. I have not passed on the message from the little boy to anyone personally, as I do not know who the mother is, but for any readers who can relate to this, the message is for you. We cannot minimize what we learn, for whether for us specifically or for another, it holds valuable energy for us and for others.

So often we think that our life is too "crowded" and that anything more would be uncomfortable. This relates to our beliefs, attitudes, and behaviors. We do not think that there is enough "room on our bench" for anything beyond our present experiences. Yet we may well be taught in numerous ways with numerous spiritual guides. One may stand out for us but, as guides are representing Truth, they are One, only in different forms. This Oneness is evidenced by my monk and the stranger speaking a common language, the language of Universal

Love. We want to learn that language—but we may not hear it spoken if we do not make room. We need to be open to embrace all that comes to us.

My Plans for Salvation

∞

October 29, 2001

Harriet Lerner's Dance of Anger has started me thinking about ideas around relationships. Who are you really angry with? The author suggests that you go back at least three generations to determine patterns or possible reasons for behavior based on number of siblings, birth order, deaths, illnesses, and so forth. I talked with Mom last night about her grandparents as well as Dad's. My family connections seem to play a part in my meditation today on Nokomis.

> I find myself on a set of steep stairs, so steep that I have to climb down backwards. As I go down, the walls close in and become narrower and narrower. I am in a tunnel. At the bottom, I start to crawl on my hands and knees, but it continues to narrow. I have to drag myself along on my belly. A series of turns takes me to a dead end. It is black. I carefully edge my way backwards. There

is no place to turn around and crawl forward, and the way is difficult. I am upset with myself for taking the stairs down.

Finally, I see a faint light and follow another tunnel toward it. This tunnel comes out on a cliff with sheer walls above and below me. I catch my breath. I can't turn around because the opening is only as wide as my shoulders. But I have to go back; there is no other way. I crawl backwards, but I cut my leg. I head back to the opening.

I see an eagle right before my eyes, hovering centimeters from my face. Its eyes blink. I know I have no choice. I stick out my arm, and the eagle grabs it with a talon. I wriggle out, and he grabs my leg.

The eagle carries me across the gully to a trail and says, "You're welcome."

I know I would be safe just to follow the trail, but I head over the bank, down into the gully. I find myself in a military headquarters. The captain is sitting at a large desk, and I hand him my plans, rolled up like a scroll. He unrolls them and says, "Excellent, very good."

I go through a door onto a battlefield. There are rows and rows of wounded everywhere. I hear that I am to find all the wounded people that I know—both alive and those who have passed on. I talk with my dad, a sister, and an aunt. I see a hand waving at me in the distance. I make my way over, past rows of "soldiers."

When I arrive, I see myself as a child. I am wearing a light green chiffon dress with small, raised white polka dots. It is very short, and I have white ankle socks on. My hair is in a pageboy, and I have slightly bucktoothed teeth from sucking my thumb.

"Hello," I say. "What's your name?"

"Sandi, but I spell it with a circle over the "i." What's your name?"

"My name's Sandi too. Are you by yourself?" I ask.

"Yes, everyone else is at choir practice."

"Are you afraid?" I ask.

"No."

Her face comes right up level with me so that our eyes are directly in front of each other.

"We have the same eyes," she says. "Do we see the same things?"

"Yes."

"Are you happy?" she asks.

"Most of the time," I answer.

"Make it right for me," she says. "Do the right thing."

My bald eagle comes along and flies me across to the monastery. I meet with my guide, and we sit on the bench.

"Who made this bench?" I ask.

"Your maternal grandfather made that flower," he answers.

I kneel down and look closely at the intricate flower my grandfather has beautifully carved. When I look closer, I see there are many of these flowers.

"Who made all these other flowers?" I ask.

"Many people you know—or know about."

"The eagle that brought me over here talked to me," I say.

"We all talk the same language. The language of love is the basis, but sometimes it is the most difficult to learn," he says.

I want to go into the monastery. When we arrive, a wedding is taking place. A wedding at the monastery seems so unusual.

"We don't get many weddings here. Most people here are married to their spirituality. But sometimes we have people become married physically and spiritually. It is incredibly beautiful."

Everyone here is so very happy. He says it is wonderful if we become connected spiritually and physically.

My Interpretation

I begin by descending a steep set of stairs—descending deep into my Self. It is a very difficult process. The tunnel is far more challenging than any I have encountered before. I feel stuck, alone, and unsure of how I am going to get out. When I am at the tunnel's edge, I am not able to get further by myself. But I am always given what I need. Today, an eagle is my guide, and he flies me to my battlefield of my ancestry, to my learning. In Native American teachings, eagle medicine is the power of Great Spirit, our connection with the Divine. In *Medicine Cards,* Jamie Sams and David Carson write:

> In learning to fiercely attack your personal fear of the unknown, the wings of your soul will be supported by the ever-present breezes which are the breath of the Great Spirit . . . Within the realm of Mother Earth and Father Sky, the dance that leads to flight involves the conquering of fear and the willingness to join in the adventure that you are co-creating with the Divine. (Sams and Carson, 1999, 41-42)

I hand over my plans to the commander. They are "excellent, very good," but I do not know what they are for or what they say. I do not realize that they are plans for my salvation, for my awareness of Who I am, plans created by the Divine.

My ancestors and my past offer clues for my healing. I talk briefly with some family members for the first time in a meditation, beginning to see them through vision (but unaware of this at the time). Most important in this battlefield is my interaction with myself as a child, my inner child. We see the same things, and she wants me to make it right for her—for me to do the right thing. I do not know what she is asking me to do, but I remember her words. She plays a very large role in my future growth. My connection to my ancestors continues as my guide shows me an intricate carving by my maternal grandfather of a flower on the stone bench.

I am taught that the language of love is the basis of all of our communication, our interaction. Yet it is often the most difficult to learn because we live in the ego mind. Learning the language of love requires understanding of all aspects of our *Being*—spiritual, emotional, mental, and physical. When we are living from our ego self, we lose this interconnection to our Self.

How Do We Bring This into Our Lives?

Perhaps one the greatest blocks to uncovering our Self is the fear that, if we go rummaging through our past, we will enter this blackness and not be able to get out. We fear being consumed by the darkness that we perceive as our pain and misery and reliving every bad memory and experience of our lives. As we walk this human life, we face wounds of some sort or another. Seeing patterns in our ancestry and understanding our own past give us the framework to begin our healing. When we descend the stairs and search for the light that is there, guidance will take us to where we can safely begin the next stage of our journey to our Self. Most of us will likely need to venture "down these stairs" numerous times. This journey becomes easier when we *know* that we will be "flown" somewhere we need to go in order to learn how we can address, cleanse, and heal our wounds.

We do not create the plans for our salvation or even need to know them—we just have to *engage* in the process of Self-discovery. We need to look closely at the life and circumstances of our ancestors because the family tree holds much for our path to healing.

Getting Naked, Experiencing Love

∞

November 21, 2001

I am at home, getting settled to meditate with the singing bowls music playing.

I relax into meditation but my stomach is sore. I concentrate on getting energy through my arms and hands to my stomach. It helps immediately, but when I move on to other thoughts, a slight pain comes back.

I begin by asking questions. How do I feel? What do I want? I decide that this isn't a question-and-answer period, and I let my mind go free.

> I am alone at the river I had to swim across before when the stepping stones disappeared. I walk along the bank to see if I can find a place to cross. A large tree has fallen across, but it is high—and I am afraid of falling in. I decide to take off my clothes and swim across.

When I look at myself naked, I am beautiful. The water is warm and inviting. The rapids are massaging my body. It feels so good. I step out onto the opposite bank without my clothes and see my guide.

"Do I look the same?" I ask him.

"Yes."

"But I don't have any clothes on."

"I see clothes," he says.

We walk along and see other people. I feel a bit self-conscious.

"Can't they see that I'm naked?"

"No," he says.

In a marketplace, we see men playing the singing bowls. I walk taller and prouder in my new, beautiful body, knowing that I look clothed to everyone else.

I see the monastery across the valley and decide to use a bridge today. I try to be brave and just step out over the ledge, but I still need to hang on to a tree branch (even though I know it won't hold me if I fall). I land on a very narrow bridge. It is only as wide as a plank and has mesh going up the sides. I have to walk one foot in front of the other. It is dark. I meet a horse and rider coming from the opposite direction. I try to turn around and go back but realize I can't. I squeeze over to the left and let them by. Neither of us says anything.

I come to a fork in the bridge—to the left the bridge becomes wider and full of sunlight; to the right, it remains narrow and dark. I decide to take the right path, and I continue on in silence for some time.

I finally arrive in a very dark room or cave. There is a momentary beam of light, and I can make out a very old woman in the corner in an armchair. I walk over to her. She tells me that she is blind and doesn't need the light to see.

Just at that time, I hear water in the CD music. I have never noticed it before. It sounds like bubbles from a scuba diver.

"You have been living beneath the water. It is not natural. You cannot survive there," she says.

"But on my way here, I was in the water, and it was a beautiful and satisfying physical and emotional feeling," I respond.

"Yes, but you were on the surface. You could breathe and feel the warmth of the sun. Now you are hearing the sound of artificial breathing in a place not meant for you."

I leave and close the door behind me.

I am again naked with my beautifully formed body. I feel aroused and lie down. The wind gently whips around me. Again my physical feelings are strong. There is no one around. I am aware of a pleasure—not a physical, sexual pleasure, just a warmness.

I am then back in a crowd, naked but still no one seems to notice. I move away and lie down in the warm sun. I can see the heat of the sun caressing my body, just like heat waves off of pavement in the summer sun. It feels wonderful.

I see the monastery and know I have to get there. I am now dressed in a white robe. I take a running leap over the edge, knowing I will land on a bridge. It is a grassy pathway. I fall slightly as I land and then run as fast as I can, stumbling a couple of times, to the monastery.

I arrive totally out of breath, hardly able to speak. I meet my guide.

"I wasn't wearing any clothes, but nobody noticed. My body was so beautiful."

"You have to love yourself in all aspects before you can love anyone else. You knew that your body looked the same to others, but it was as beautiful as it could be in your eyes. You walked tall and proud with this knowledge."

"I had several erotic images even though I didn't experience sexual pleasure. I usually only feel sensations such as heat, joy, and sadness when I'm in these places," I say.

"You feel love just as you feel the other emotions. Only a small part of the love emotion is sexual. It is mostly the feeling of warmth and tenderness. Most of our loving relationships are not sexual. You felt true love. You loved yourself, and you could love others. It is the universal love.

"That rainbow we see over there is flawless. It is beautiful. But that yellow isn't as bright as it usually is, just as sometimes can be the case with humans. As individuals, we may not be perfect, but humanity is full of love and is flawless."

As I head home, I come to the stream. I notice a long rope hanging from the trees. I swing across the river and land on the other side.

MY INTERPRETATION

The river is a metaphor for the challenges we face and, more important, the lessons we have learned from them on our journey to "cross over" to our Higher Self, to *living* our Higher Self. In a previous meditation (see "What Looks Easy Is Not Always So"), I thought that my swim across the river would be straightforward. I took off only some of my clothes—and only partially committed to this transition. In the meditation today, I recognize this river, remember the problems I had, and look for another way to get around it. I still do not want to enter it, to face it. But when I see no option, I get naked. I have learned that I need to "take my clothes off," become naked. I now have fully committed to this journey, I *become* my Higher Self and *experience* the Love that I am.

This transition requires that we leave behind things of this world, leave behind all our ego beliefs, all our fears. By "taking off" these things, I uncover Who I am, uncloak my Self, and experience a most wonderful, physically sensual feeling. I feel it again when I am lying in the wind and with the warmth of the sun. With this connection to my Self, I see my body as most beautiful. I feel Unconditional Love as a most pleasing, warm, physical sensation. I *feel* love of myself and so can love others.

But I am self-conscious in being naked, being exposed. I do not want to be seen as different; I am embarrassed about being spiritual. At this time, I am extremely private about what has been happening to me, fearful of how I will look. Moreover, I do not really understand the meaning of what I am experiencing. But my guide tells me he sees clothes and that others see me as clothed. It is only then that am I able to walk tall and proud in Who I am. While I look the same to others, I know I am more beautiful than ever. My Inner Beauty is shining forth. This is how I feel and experience life when I *live* as my Higher Self while in this body. When I return to cross the river, there is a rope. I am now my Self, clothed for this world in a white robe of the crown chakra. I easily cross back into this world with the knowledge that I am a Divine Being.

For the first bridge today, I want to be brave and have trust, but I still have an inkling of doubt as I hang on to a branch, even knowing that it will be of no use. I am recognizing that things of this world will not save me. The bridge is narrow and dark, and I meet a horse and rider.

I am the rider on the horse, but I am unable to turn around and go with them. I am then given the choice of taking the sunny, wider fork, but I take the narrow, dark one. In a previous meditation (see "A

Stranger"), I was on a scary bridge—and my guide had me leave it. It was not for me. Here I am learning to intuitively know which bridge to take, often the dark path, so as to see, understand, and grow from what is in that darkness.

I come upon a dark room where a momentary beam of light reveals a very old, wise woman in the corner. She is blind, but she sees with vision—not with her eyes. She tells me that I have been living artificially and cannot survive like this. This state is not natural. *A Course in Miracles* says:

> Grace is the natural state of every Son of God. When he is not in a state of grace, he is out of his environment and does not function well. Everything he does becomes a strain, because he was not created for the environment that he has made. (*ACIM*, 1996, 136)

The scuba diving metaphor illustrates this well. Regardless of whether we are operating in our ego mind, we are always surrounded by, and part of, God, Source Energy, our True Nature—here symbolized as water. As a scuba diver, I have been living with the ego belief that I am not part of the ocean but separate from it—and separate from every other "scuba diver." I live artificially because I believe in that which I am not—separate. Scuba divers are always concerned about their air, the quality of that air, whether they are too deep, how long they can stay down, and how fast they rise. The air in the tank will always run out. Even if they become very comfortable diving (see themselves as comfortable as their separate self), there are always the precautions necessary for the "what ifs." "What ifs" will always happen; we live in a state of varying degrees of fear.

I learn to trust completely that there will always be a bridge for me. Over time, my trust has grown bit by bit as I try to find these bridges and take a step onto them. As I make my way to my final bridge today, I am symbolically dressed in a white robe of Divine Awareness; I let go of any fear and fully trust. As I land on this bridge, it is unlike any of the others I have encountered. It is not narrow or dark or high; it is a safe, grassy pathway, alive with growth. I run back to what I see as my "spiritual home," sometimes stumbling but anxious to arrive.

How Do We Bring This into Our Lives?

We become truly naked. This has nothing to do with physical nakedness, which is relatively easy; it is being naked in our Soul. By stripping down all that "covers" us, we find true love of ourselves, and, as an extension, of others. It is where we can live without the ego strangleholds of image or loneliness or pain from any number of sources. To become naked in this sense requires that we strip down everything of the ego, everything that we hold dear that "belongs" to this world. When we do, the swim across the river to our Higher Self will be blissful. Perhaps we need to start with baby steps and let go of just one thing that we think we cannot live without. When we find that we can, letting go of the next—and then the next—becomes easier and easier, until we can give up the last trappings of our unforgiving thoughts.

If we do not "cross the river" to know our Divine Being, we are living unnaturally; the sustenance of our body's life—breathing—is artificial. Our natural state is Grace. When we believe we are separate, even though we *are* Grace, we have put up barriers that require constant upkeep, constant vigilance, and, implicit within them, constant fear. We need to take off our "scuba tanks" to understand that we are living in Spirit that embraces us, envelops us, and infuses us with the peace and tranquility of *being* a particle of the ocean. There is nothing stronger than water. We are Grace.

As individuals, we make mistakes. If we think of the seven billion people on earth as individuals, then there will be seven billion egos making mistakes. But if, through Unconditional Love, we understand their True Essence, and ours, then we will see these seven billion people as flawless and perfect.

My View from Three Eyes

∞

December 5, 2001

I split my appointment between a massage and Reiki. By the end of the massage, I am very relaxed and am with my guide.

> We are in a meadow on a wide dirt road. We walk along the road, and I tell him that I don't feel quite deep enough, that I need to wait for my Reiki Master to start the treatment. My guide and I wait patiently for her.
>
> My Reiki Master begins.
>
> My guide and I continue to walk in the meadow, but there is nothing around. I tell him that I feel that I still need to go deeper.
>
> My Reiki Master is now at my chest, and I silently ask her for help.

I can feel sunbeams enter my body through my chest. It is like in a movie when you see someone's spirit enter or leave their body.

My guide asks me to isolate my heart, and I am easily able to. "That is your lifeline," he says.

"Now isolate your kidneys," he instructs. I have a bit more trouble, but I find them.

"Isolate your right eye." No problem. "Turn this eye around and look inside your head." I see a factory arranged like a multi-layered library. People are working individually, facing the wall. "Are they happy?" he asks me. They seem to be. "Take a closer look." I focus on two people; one is mending a hole in the wall, and the other is hammering a board across a hole.

"Turn your right eye back to the front and isolate your left eye." As with my right eye, I am able to turn it around and look inside. I am in a classroom and see myself as a young girl, but I don't recognize the other students or the teacher. It is very quiet; everyone is working while the teacher writes on the board. I go into the hall, but there is no one around. Everyone else is still working quietly in the classroom. I walk along for a while, and then everyone comes running out of the classrooms. I go back into "my" classroom, into the quiet. My guide tells me to turn my left eye back around.

"You have a third eye," he says. "Find it and look out."

I see a huge kaleidoscope, mostly yellow at first, but then all sorts of colors. He asks me to turn my third eye around and look inside. It is very foggy, and I can't see anything. He has me turn my third eye back around.

A loud bell rings in the music, and we are at the monastery. All the monks are filing along in rows, but they look rather morose.

"What's happened?" I ask.

"They are going to a funeral," he responds.

I remember the last time I saw them (see "My Plans for Salvation") they were celebrating at a wedding. My guide tells me that they know the Spirit is going on to a good place.

We are back on the road in the meadow. I feel that we are wandering.

A man comes up from behind and asks if I know somewhere to eat, that he is very hungry. I look around and see a village to the left. I point it out, and he asks if I can take him there.

We walk along and arrive at a village where everyone is riding donkeys. When they see us, they are ecstatic. I feel like Mary and Joseph entering Bethlehem, although I don't see the man, "my Joseph," again.

As I am led to a tent, everyone continues to be excited by my presence. A group of women huddle around a younger woman who has been beaten by her husband, which is not uncommon here. I find her husband. He, too, knows about me, but he is not afraid. I ask him why he has beaten his wife, and he says he didn't like the way she had looked at him. I slap him across the face. He is amazed and asks why I hit him.

"I didn't like the way you looked at me." I hit him again and give him the same reason. "If you don't want someone to do something to you, don't do it to them. Do unto others as you would have them do unto you."

He is so apologetic that, much to the initial fear of the women, he goes to the tent and finds his wife.

He hugs her, cleans her wound, and says that he will never do that again. Although he thinks it might be difficult to find a way to change the attitudes of other men that allows them to still maintain face, he is going to find a way.

Then, back at the monastery, my guide and I are among all the monks. We hold hands, and I can feel their power. They look happy, and my guide tells me that this is because I have come so far; they have gained a new soul. Because when one soul becomes stronger or at peace, everyone becomes more at peace.

My guide tells me that I will be all right. I have much support. He wants me to keep coming back to him. We sit on the bench and take in the beauty of the sights. He wants me to look with my third eye. I see a yellow circle about the size of a quarter. I turn the eye inward and see something. I can't remember what it is though.

My Interpretation

We have "three eyes" from which to see, and which eye we use will determine our view of the world we live in. With our right eye, we see the world of the ego, the world of separation, where everyone is working alone, stacked in layers (society's hierarchy of perceived importance). I think they are happy, but when I take a closer look, they are fixing things, covering holes. Everything is always breaking and in need of repairs. This is our life as a separate self.

When we look with our left eye (through meditation, religious practice, spiritual reading), we enter our classroom of Truth. There are many classrooms—some are filled with students, and some for self-learning—but they are all in this same "structure for Higher Learning." One classroom is no better than another; one (or perhaps several) will resonate more for each of us. I am more comfortable in the classroom of independent study, a foreshadowing of my learning through *A Course in Miracles*.

As we continue to learn in our classroom, we begin to see with our third eye in the middle of our forehead. We see with vision, with the eyes of our Divine Self. Things outside of us now look different; we no longer look upon this world as we once did. I see a kaleidoscope of colors, colors of the chakras. Looking inward will be equally different—from the shame, blame, and fear of our ego selves to the awareness of our Divine Perfection. I am as yet unable to see inside to my Self—everything is still misted over. However, at the end, I look out and see a yellow circle, the color of the third chakra. When I look inside, I see something, but I cannot remember. The third chakra (the "last chakra of the body") is associated with developing ourselves as individuals, a relationship with ourselves rather than with others in the second chakra and our families in the first.

In *Anatomy of the Spirit: The Seven Stages of Power and Healing*, Caroline Myss says:

> This [*third chakra*] energy center also contains most issues related to the development of personal power and self-esteem.
>
> The third chakra completes the physical trilogy of the human energy system. Like chakras one and two, it primarily relates to a physical form of power. Where the first chakra resonates to group or tribal power, and the where the second resonates to the flow of power between the self and others, the third chakra relates to our personal power in relation to the external world. (Myss, 1996, 167)

Having been led to see with vision, I am asked to perform a miracle, as "miracles arise from a mind that is ready for them" (*ACIM*, 1996, 10). I enter a town with a stranger and feel like we are Mary and Joseph. At the time, I think that I am not Mary, that I am just myself playing a part in a vision. But awareness of Christ-consciousness is growing within me, and so I am with Grace to perform miracles.

In this village, abuse is the norm. Do we blame or judge the husband for beating his wife? This is how he has been conditioned. This does not make it right, but it allows for non-judgment and moves us out of ego. *A Course in Miracles* says:

> You respond to what you perceive, and as you perceive so shall you behave. The Golden Rule asks you to do unto others as you would have them do unto you. This means that the perception of both must be accurate. The Golden Rule is the rule for appropriate behavior. You cannot behave appropriately unless you perceive correctly. Since you and your neighbor are equal members of one family, as you perceive both so you will do to both. (*ACIM*, 1996, 10)

I perform a miracle to change the perception of one man, and, through him, others. My slap is the miracle, the catalyst for him to see and experience differently. I open the man to see Oneness, and, in understanding this, to change himself and attempt to change others. It will not be easy, but he sees differently. Change is possible—one person at a time—but it must first be with ourselves. Change comes from non-judgment and understanding—from seeing with vision. The monks see me as one who, by changing myself, will change others.

I am shown how the monks are fully engaged in the passages and experiences of life. Here, they are saddened by the death of another. Before (see "My Plans for Salvation"), they were joyous at a wedding. We are to be fully present in this life journey regardless of how it tugs at our emotions.

How Do We Bring This into Our Lives?

We have the option of choosing which of our eyes we use to look upon something—whether it is an object, a person, a behavior, or a change in a situation. We can look with logic and try to slot everything into the world of duality—good or bad, right or wrong, and so forth. Or we can look with our creative side and perceive possible learning from situations. Or, finally, we could go further and learn to see with our third eye, with the eye of our Soul, our Higher Self. It is with such vision that we see the outside through a kaleidoscope of intricate designs and colors, of the interconnectedness of all we look upon. On the inside, we see our True Self—we see ourselves as the Divine Beings that we are.

How do we react to "slaps" that jar us from our routines, beliefs, habits? Do these slaps wake us up to the fact that we are not living true to our Self? These may be a job loss, a failed relationship, an illness, burnout, a death, something that questions our beliefs and judgments, or a suggestion from another that our behavior is inappropriate or our words are hurtful. Do we try to defend ourselves against these slaps? Do we rationalize them? Do we try to ignore them? Do we fight back? Do we belittle them? Do we fall victim to them? Or do we see these slaps as the miracles they are—to wake us up to look closely at our beliefs, behavior, life situation, and see what needs to be changed for our own good? They are indeed a great gift. Sometimes when we change ourselves, we encounter resistance from others; it can disrupt their individual paradigms. But we need to stay steadfast in our commitment to our new awareness.

In this life, we will face joys and sorrows. We cannot escape the reality of sorrow. We need to fully embrace all that life presents us: to feel it, experience it, but not wallow in it. Wallowing involves attachment to the loss, such that it defines us. Grieving is being with the pain, accepting it, and honoring the time and space it takes to live fully in spite of any loss.

The City of Gold

∞

December 12, 2001

I have a very different vision during my Reiki treatment; I don't like my experience at all at the beginning.

> I am in a very dark room. The singing bowls music seems very loud and is irritating. At first, I am crawling along on all fours, and then on my belly, but I do not see any lights or passageways to get out. I tell myself to feel around and find out where I am. But instead, I just sit there. I can't see anything. I stick out my tongue to try to taste something—but nothing. I can only hear the music, which seems very loud.
>
> My Reiki Master moves to my throat chakra.
>
> I sense a person with me, but that person doesn't answer when I call. I soon feel as though someone is turning my head up and to the side. I feel so much pain. My

neck is so sore that I am finding it difficult to breathe. My throat seems to be closing off. I have never before felt such a strong physical reaction in a meditation, and I briefly wonder if I am going to be all right.

When my Reiki Master moves to my heart chakra, the pain seems to abate. I move my head slightly to lessen the pain. I am still in the dark room, but I'm not moving or trying to get out. Why is someone not helping me?

I completely break down in tears on the table. I am sobbing uncontrollably. My Reiki Master asks if I am all right, and I nod. My crying continues for some time until finally the sobs lessen.

Why isn't anyone helping me get out? Why am I not trying to find a way?

Finally, I see a crack of light above me. The opening is narrow and almost straight up. I feel around and find rungs to climb. I poke through the small hole onto a huge grassy meadow. I lie on my back and dangle my knees and feet over the hole to rest and breathe. When I get up and stretch, I am stiff from sitting so long, and my neck still aches. I look around, but there is nothing to be seen.

Shortly, I notice birds flying overhead and then a bald eagle. He flies off, comes back, circles around, and takes off again in the same direction. He repeats this several times. My eyes are tired, and I have to concentrate to calm them. I close my eyes. I see the eagle's eye looking so intently at me. He tells me to follow him. I do, but I can't keep up. He circles back and picks me up. We are flying through the air, and it is beautiful. I tell him I have been in a very sad place. He just keeps flying, and I focus on the beauty around me.

He drops me into a huge deciduous tree with no leaves. I look down and see a person on the ground, leaning against the tree and eating an apple.

I start to climb down, but just before the bottom, I knock an apple on his head.

"Oh hello," he says. "I'm glad you're here."

"Where are we?" I ask.

"This is a very special tree. People come here from all over."

"What kind of tree is it?"

"This tree is anything you want it to be. Today, I came to it as a good luck tree, and here you are. You are my good luck. What did you come for today?"

"I guess I have come for direction."

"This is the best place for direction because any way you look is open and available to you. Any direction you take includes possible pathways beside it," he says.

I look around to see what direction I will take. The sun is directly overhead; I can't tell north, south, east, or west. I take off in a direction and ask him to join me. He offers me an apple, and it tastes so good. He talks the whole time, but I'm not sure about what because I am still remembering the pain when I was in the room.

Finally, we arrive at a large river. He says that he can't go any further, and we say good-bye. I look at the large river and think, *Not again.* I swim across—there isn't much of a current—but at the other side, I am angry. What if someone doesn't know how to swim! Why does everything have to be so difficult! I get up and wave to my friend.

"Good-bye and thank you," I yell.

"No, thank you," he says.

I wave off my anger at the "water challenge" and climb the grassy bank. I look down upon a huge, beautiful city that glitters in gold. Everything is shimmering in the sunlight. I make my way down to the city and find everyone incredibly friendly.

"Hello, hello," everyone keeps saying.

I see apples at a stall. They are gold. Someone buys one, and when he bites into it, it becomes a bright red apple. I put my hand on the gold wall, and I can see the "real" bricks. People's faces are flesh, but their clothes are made of gold. All the inanimate objects are gold.

People ask if I have somewhere to stay. When I say no, they tell me to come with them. We enter a warm, friendly room. Everyone there begins to touch my face and arms, and they give me wonderful compliments. I ask why people's faces are not gold. They tell me that, when someone is loved, their True Self is revealed. It is the reverse of Midas. "Everything he touched turned to gold. That is wrong. We are all as beautiful as gold, and love will bring us out to our full beauty."

They have me look in a mirror. My face and arms are gold. I haven't had enough love. When someone touches my face, my skin becomes visible.

"How long does it take to 'keep' your skin?" I ask.

"It depends upon how much love you need. It changes for all people. Look at the older man in the chair," they say. "He is the master." He absolutely glows, and light encircles his whole face.

I leave the City of Gold and thank everyone for their help. They were so comforting. I climb a small knoll and look out to the monastery. I meet my guide, and we sit on the bench. I ask him why he hadn't been there for me when I was in the dark room, unable to move and in pain. He tells me that I was pushing out to grow—like a tree seed or a young chick in an egg. They are nurtured until they are ready to grow and flourish.

"You are like that. You have come alive from a dormant state, woken from hibernation after the winter frost. You are ready to grow and see, feel, hear, and touch all the beauty of the world. Everything around you is the same, but you see it differently."

He takes my hand as we sit on the bench. He tells me that I am going to be all right—and that I have all the help I need.

I feel at peace.

My Interpretation

In the previous meditation (see "My View from Three Eyes"), I feel that people saw me as Mary entering Bethlehem, and now I am told that I *am* as Mary, birthing my Higher Self, birthing the Christ within me. My guide tells me that my difficult, lonely, paralyzing time in the dark room, and then my experience of the very painful twisting of my neck, are the symbolic birthing of the Christ within. I am awakening from slumber in this world, from the ego, to awareness of my True Self. My ego wants nothing of this birth, this transition. It does not want me to see or experience anything but its intricate facade of its self. With my entry into the world of Spirit through my meditations, the dormant, unconscious knowledge within me is moving to consciousness.

My head feels like it is being completely twisted off of my body. My throat chakra is closed. My ego is fighting to keep control and almost wins. I nearly end the meditation because of the pain. It would be unbearable if it did not let up.

The throat chakra is the breaking point of the ego. When this chakra is open, the ego is no longer in control of the mind. In *A*

- *Handbook of Chakra Healing: Spiritual Practice for Health, Harmony, and Inner Peace,* Kalashatra Govinda writes:

    > The throat chakra lies near the larynx and leads the way to the highest chakras . . . it connects the heart and forehead chakra [*third eye*] and is thus responsible for balancing the worlds of feeling and thought . . . What we say to others, and above all what we say to ourselves, influences our mental world and our feelings about life. (Govinda, 2002, 31-32)

Do we hear and speak from our heart and third eye—from the Truth and Will of God? Or do we hear and speak from our brain—from the truth and will of our ego? The Will of God is in direct opposition to our ego's will, which believes that we are in control of everything in our lives. Everything we have been taught—and everything we experience in this world—is jeopardized by understanding Who we truly are.

As through all darkness, a glimmer of light appears, but I must climb out alone. There is no rescuer to carry me out. I must make the first move—and have the willingness to walk forward toward the light, toward my Soul. In just that willingness, Divine Guidance gives me direction, guidance, and help.

My direction today comes from the Great Spirit eagle. But progress is slow by myself, and I cannot keep up. And so I fly with the eagle, and with him, see the beauty around me. We can walk our journey alone, but our progress will be easier and faster with help.

The eagle drops me into a tree, a tree that people come to for whatever they need. I call it the Tree of Wisdom; symbolically it is the place where we are connected to Divine Knowledge. For me, I am given direction to the teachings of the City of Gold.

A man has come to the tree for good luck. I drop an apple on his head, which parallels the story of Newton's discovery of gravity. Why Newton? What does his presence have to teach me? Newton was inspired to understand gravity and how everything is connected to the sun by this gravitational force; we are all connected by the power of the

Divine. Newton's presence is a way of telling me that when we come to this place of Oneness, here symbolized by the tree, we discover much about Truth.

Newton is talking to me our entire time together, but I am unable to listen because I can only think of my previous pain—even though it does not hurt any longer. Since I am living in the past, which is the ego, I am unable to live in the present and hear the gifts that are given to me.

The tree gives me direction—direction not chosen by logic or my ego but by my Higher Self. None of my senses can determine the best way. And maybe there is not a "best way" since "best" involves judgment. Perhaps the point here is not to take the "right" way but simply to take a step. For regardless of which direction I take, there will likely be a "river" to cross. I leave Newton when it is time for me to cross another river to continue with my own learning.

Even though the river crossing is not difficult, I am angry. "Why is someone not helping me? This journey is supposed to be pleasant—certainly not painful." My angry reaction to being presented with another river to cross highlights an important aspect of our ego thoughts. Twice before I have crossed rivers. The first was when I was exhausted after needing to swim upstream when the water got deeper (see "What Looks Easy Is Not Always So"). The second was when I arrived at this same river, became naked and experienced the bliss of my Self (see "Getting Naked, Experiencing Love"). Yet today, I immediately associate having to cross the river with my first, unpleasant experience—completely "forgetting" my blissful second one. This is what we so often do. Our fear first propels us to pain and trials of the past. We will continue to face challenges until we are living totally with our Higher Self. We need to be conscious of being paralyzed by fearing the worst—reliving the past—rather than moving forward with awareness that we will safely cross any river we are guided to. These challenges become less and less difficult over time when we walk with our Self.

The City of Gold is a wonderful metaphor for our ego self and Higher Self—or the materialistic world and the world of Divine Love and Compassion. Our ego self sees worth as gold—something outside of us, a commodity used to compare all value, accumulate wealth, achieve status, and determine all aspects of our personal worth. We are living the myth of King Midas. Significantly, his "gift" causes his death when his food turns to hardened gold when he touches it—and he cannot eat. We need to see with vision what is enduring—and what has true value. The people living in the City of Gold know they *are* Love and freely give that Love to others. They are spiritual beings in a material world; anything they touch turns into what they need. Abundance is theirs.

My face and arms are gold because I am living in the world of the ego. It is through the touch of Unconditional Love that the gold disappears and reveals my True Self. At the time, I think that my lack of love refers to a lack of love from others. But I now understand it is my lack of love for myself. I am Love. I see the glow of radiance from the Master and feel the Love around. I am with my Higher Self when my body is flesh.

How Do We Bring This into Our Lives?

This meditation begins with an example of how our ego can work to block Self-discovery. We want to heal and live with Inner Peace, but it can be uncomfortable when we begin the process. It is dark, frightening, and painful—so much so that we abandon our attempts. *I can't do it. It's not worth it. It's too painful. I'm fine the way I am. I don't need this.*

If we experience this, we just need to know there is a light. If we just get up and walk, there will be all the help we need to receive guidance and direction for our learning. We need not *expect* these difficult experiences, but if we do experience them, they present great learning. We will be all right. We need to trust in the process—and not let the past dictate our present moments or let our ego voice that assumes the worse determine our peace.

We tend to always want to go the best way or make the best choice when we are discovering our Self. Whichever way we go will take us to our lesson. Sometimes, we will be drawn in a particular way; sometimes, we just need to move in some direction, and whoever we meet along the way holds lessons for us.

It is through the touch of Unconditional Love, both giving and receiving, that we are transformed from solid, impenetrable bodies to bodies filled with the awareness of our Spirit and fully living our earthly experience. This is the real, enduring value that we seek—the value that will nourish us and bring us to awareness of Who we are. The City of Gold is teaching us to live in this world as spiritual beings, receiving and giving love.

Never Forgotten, Just Not Remembered

∞

December 19, 2001

I am having a Reiki treatment.

> I am on a white horse, wearing a suit of armor and a helmet. We are in a misty, enchanted forest with bare and gnarled trees. It is dark, either early dawn or late dusk. The music playing seems eerie. Owls are hooting. I don't know where to go.
>
> I am uncomfortable because I don't know how to ride. I get off the horse. Eventually, a woman comes by. Like the good witch in *The Wizard of Oz*, she has a wand, long blonde hair, and a beautiful gown.
>
> "I am here to help you relax," she says.
>
> "Are you like a guide?" I ask her.
>
> "We have many guides. I am here to calm you."

She puts her hands over my eyes, and they immediately relax. I go into a deeper sense of calm.

"My stomach also needs help," I say.

She places her hand over my stomach and wiggles her fingers. I can see the problem coming out in waves. It is amazing to watch.

"What is your name?" I ask.

"Glinda."

I struggle to get on my horse, and I tell her I don't know how to ride.

"You never forget," she says.

I then easily mount the horse and ride off through the forest into a meadow that soon ends with a sheer cliff to the valley below. There is no way I am going to try to jump across the canyon, horse or no horse, meditation or no meditation!

I dismount and lead my horse along the edge. Eventually, I see what looks like a very narrow pathway down into the canyon. I lead my horse through all the hairpin turns. I am worried that he will fall because he is so much bigger and doesn't know the full danger. I come to a particularly narrow spot. I know the horse will never make it across without falling, but I find two handholds above me and make a "wall" with my body on the outside. The horse squeezes between the canyon wall and me and makes it safely past.

As we proceed, the horse stumbles a couple of times but manages to regain its balance. I then realize with such clarity that the four legs of the horse represent my four children. I am leading them through this peril, trying to protect them. They were trying to help each other out when they stumbled. I look at the legs with love. My horse and I continue to the bottom and enter a damp, dark passageway. I hear water dripping from the ceiling. We slowly make our way along. Once through this uncomfortable passageway, we exit into the bright sun, only to see the monastery.

I am now with my children, and we arrive at the monastery. I introduce them to my guide. They all run off and start playing happily with other children. I climb up an extremely steep slope. I feel as though I am going to fall backwards. At the top, I look down upon the monastery.

My guide says, "You have reached a higher plane. The monastery is wonderful, but this is better."

I climb back down, show the children the bench, and have them look at its beauty. They are happy and I know they will be all right. We set off, waving good-bye to my guide.

My Interpretation

I am in an eerie place, wearing full armor. I believe that I need to protect myself in this frightening place, in this world I live in. I am uncomfortable on the horse because I do not know how to ride. I *am* actually quite uncomfortable with horses—despite not really ever having been near them. The reason for this will become clear in time.

Glinda is another guide; she calms me and extracts something from my stomach that is not good for me. More important, she tells me that we never forget what we already know—we always know Who we are.

Horses have appeared in two previous meditations. In "A Pot of Gold," I see a horse without a rider and am taught that I have been living inside a tornado. In "Getting Naked, Experiencing Love," I land on a narrow plank bridge and have to move aside for a horse and rider going in the opposite direction. In both of these meditations, the horse is going the opposite way, and I am being told that I am out of harmony with my Self—living in the eye of a tornado and living artificially under the water.

In the meditation today, I am riding this horse; I am going with him, in the same direction, but life still presents obstacles to overcome. During my vigilant caring for the horse, I am able to understand that it symbolizes my four children. I am there to guide them, help them when they stumble, and—once through the challenges—introduce them to my guide, a representative of my growing awareness. As they happily play and experience my journey, I understand that they will be fine.

I climb above the monastery to go beyond—but not without a very uncomfortable feeling of falling. To proceed beyond where I have been seems difficult, but the "view" from above gives great perspective. By first including my children, by sharing my experiences, I come to a "height" that surpasses where I have been. Sharing our experiences benefits us all.

How Do We Bring This into Our Lives?

We have always known our True Self, we have always known Who we really are and how to do our life's work. However, we just do not remember that we know. If we go about our life thinking, "I know I can," we tap into this realization and move toward the *experience* of this being true.

We have such an incredible library of knowledge locked in our unconscious. Glinda is indeed the Good Witch of the North from *The Wizard of Oz*, but never in a million years would I have been able to tell you her name. Even hearing the name in the meditation, it did not register and only later, did I find the name in my research. This is just one of those little reminders that we have all we need to know within us.

When we change, those around us are affected. The effect of growing to understand one's Higher Self will be very positive for everyone. We need to be open about our Inner Spirit world, about the experiences we have on our journeys. It may seem risky or uncomfortable to reveal such a change, but if we are following our Inner Guidance, this change will not only be key for our growth—but also for the guidance and help we give, directly or indirectly, to others.

Eaten Alive

∞

December 20, 2001

I am hiking Nokomis and meditate at the top.

> I imagine my colors. Red comes first and is undulating. I then ask for yellow. The change makes it look like a film screen with red moving over to the right, and then a big yellow ball fills the screen. The same transition happens for orange. I ask for purple, but I cannot "get" it. I move to white, and it fills the screen.
>
> I find myself in a desert under my same tree that gives me direction. I am so tired. *Let me just sleep for a few minutes.* I feel myself go into a sleep.
>
> I wake up to a vulture staring me in the face, waiting to peck away if I remain still or die. I stand up immediately and drive him away. I feel fortunate that I woke up in time. I then notice a quarter-sized raw gash in my

right leg below the back of my knee. I realize that the vulture has been pecking away at me, eating my flesh, without my knowledge or sensation. But now, I can feel some pain and am limping.

I start heading out from the tree, in no particular direction, across the desert. A man on a camel comes up over a small knoll.

"Where are you going?" he asks.

"I don't know."

"There is nothing in the direction you are going. I am going across the desert. Why don't you join me?"

He notices my wound. "You have a bad cut on your leg. You'd better take care of it."

I put a scarf around it. I try to get up on the camel, but I fall off. The camel lowers his face and looks me directly in the eye.

"You stink," I say.

"You stink too," he replies.

We stare at each other for a while. I try to get up again and succeed. I sit behind the man and hold on to his waist. We seem to ride for a long time, not talking. We eventually come to the crest of a hill and look down upon a small city. At first, I think it is the City of Gold, but I soon realize that it is not.

We enter the town on foot. I am leading and can see that the women in the town are not treated well by the men. I tell the men and women of the village to go with their partner into the bedroom and do whatever the woman wants. I empower the women, using the bedroom as a place of strength. When they come back, I ask them how it was.

"It didn't go well," they say.

"You now know how it feels to have power over another. For many, that power is addictive. But it is not supposed to be like that. Go back to the bedroom and share power in everything," I tell them.

They come back smiling, very pleased with the mutual feeling. My rider friend and I leave on the camel and continue our journey through the desert.

My Interpretation

When I am embraced in the color white, the crown chakra where the life force enters the body, I find myself at the Tree of Wisdom—a tree for direction for me. But I am too exhausted to move anywhere. I just want to sleep, thereby ignoring any decision. I fall into the sleep of the ego, the belief that I am only a body, a solitary, separate, decaying entity. I am not awake to my Higher Self and the awareness that I am the Universal Source, connected to everything and everyone, Infinite.

The imagery of this is powerful. The vulture (our beliefs that we are separate from each other and from the Divine, with all the resultant unresolved issues we face in our lives) slowly but assuredly eats away at us while we are asleep, while we are not *consciously* aware. When we live our lives in this ego state, we are not even aware of being eaten alive. We are numb to the pain our ego beliefs inflict. It is only when we wake up to our Higher Self—or the vulture (ego) has pecked away enough that we face a diseased state—that we notice our wounds. They hurt and cripple us.

I awake from my ego sleep, notice my wounds, and feel lucky to have woken up in time. However, I do nothing about it until the man tells me that I need to take care of the wound. Oftentimes, we need to hear from someone else, be they a human or spiritual angel, that we must address our wounds. If we do not, if we do not connect and resolve our emotional issues with our disease, the wound will not heal.

The man tells me that I am going the wrong way because there is nothing for me to learn in that direction. He and the camel are guiding me to another town. I am unable to get on the camel on my first attempt. I have not connected with my new guide. I am repelled by his smell. With his reply that I smell to him, that only our bodies are different, we look into each other's eyes and connect. I can now mount him. Camels are unique animals. They are able to travel great distances, storing food and water in their bodies. My camel guide is prepared to carry me on my journey, able to supply me with all that I need along the way for as long as it takes. With him, I am safe to go into my desert.

This is the second meditation where gender inequality surfaces (see "My View from Three Eyes"). Why do I have the men and women go to the bedroom? Why not the council chambers or the workplace? The bedroom is a symbol for our intimacy with another. Without a shared intimacy, a relationship does not *feel* good. But before we can connect with another, we need to be spiritually, mentally, emotionally, and physically intimate with ourselves. It is in waking up from our sleep that we are able to achieve this.

How Do We Bring This into Our Lives?

The imagery of being eaten alive by the vulture is so very poignant; it demonstrates how our emotional wounds are carried in our bodies and will manifest into cancers, chronic illnesses, or diseases—unless we wake up and drive away the "vulture." But that is not enough. We need to take care of this wound left by the vulture (abandonment, rejection, guilt, abuse, disappointment, shame, and so forth) so that we heal our pain—our internal dysfunction—through awareness of our Divine Nature.

We can do this independently, but often we need "someone" to point out that we need to dress our wounds. This someone may be spiritual books or lectures, family, friends, a counselor, an acquaintance, a chance encounter, or a spiritual path. In whatever form, they guide us to take care of ourselves and address where the wound came from—not to simply apply a Band-Aid. They help us heal from the emotional issues that have kept us captive as the living dead for the vulture to feast on.

Perhaps one of the more difficult aspects of this is going in a certain direction when we do not know why or where or how or what we are going there for. It requires trust that we are being led to exactly where we are supposed to be for the greatest benefit of ourselves and others.

We strive for intimacy in our lives. But what is intimacy? Here, we are taught that it is the balance of complete openness with another *because* we are naked, stripped down to Who we truly are. One does not have power *over* another. It must feel right—not by ego standards but by our Higher Self. And this balance is possible only if we are completely intimate with ourselves—know Who we are in all facets of our Being.

Painting Our Self-Portrait

∞

January 9, 2002

I have a short massage before Reiki, as I've been quite tense lately. The music playing sounds orchestral.

> I imagine being in a big field with the clouds moving quickly. The heavens are singing, and I hear the angels playing harps. I am then in white fluffy clouds, walking along as the angels play their harps and stringed instruments.
>
> Once my massage is finished, my Reiki Master changes the music to singing bowls.
>
> I am walking along the same path, but it changes from clouds to a forest. I feel the earth tremble in time to the music. I wonder if I am in the midst of an earthquake. As I am rocked around by the earth, I see two riders silhouetted in the distance. They are dark shapes,

they do not look menacing. I wonder who they are, and I feel a need to go deeper into meditation to find out.

I sit down, trying to calm my eyes.

My guide comes and says, "Hello."

"I've had a roller-coaster time with my emotions," I say. "The earth was trembling."

"The earth is alive. It has energy and always did. But most people don't see it or feel it."

"I'm having problems with my eyes."

"Try to 'fix' it yourself," he says.

I can't seem to, but he puts his hands over my eyes—and they immediately relax.

"Look into my eyes and see what is there," he says.

I stare into his eyes, centimeters away, but I don't see anything.

He tells me to look harder.

I try but still nothing. I close my eyes; when I reopen them, I am looking right at the eagle's eye, which then becomes my guide's eye, and back and forth they go.

"Why do I always have this difficulty calming my eyes?" I ask.

"Your eyes are very important. They allow you to see the real world," he answers.

"But what about blind people?" I ask.

"It is with your third eye that you see the real world," he says.

"Who were the two riders I saw earlier?"

"I am not only your teacher. I am your guide. I cannot tell you all the answers. I only guide you to them."

The forest is rather dark, but soon I can see the sun through the trees, rising up from the earth. I walk out into the sun and feel the warmth.

My Reiki Master moves her hands to my throat.

Again, I feel a strong twisting of my head up and to the right.

"Oh no—not again," I say.

"Work through it; you will be all right," my guide says.

"Why is this happening?"

"You must find out," he replies.

The pain increases until my Reiki Master moves her hands to my shoulders.

We continue to walk along in the sunshine. My guide is holding my right hand. This is the first time he is on this side—he's usually on my left. He lets go of my hand, and my right arm begins to feel funny. It feels heavy and light at the same time. My upper arm has some pain, and my lower arm and hand are tingling. My arm begins to levitate and detach from my body. My head detaches as well and moves to the ground beside me. My guide is just standing there watching.

My Reiki Master moves from my root chakra.

I walk over to my arm and reattach it to my shoulder. Then I go over to my head and screw it back on.

I am alone on a beautiful white sandy beach, burying my feet in the sand to warm them up. Once in a while, I run into the lapping water to cool my feet before burying them again.

I look down the beach and see a large, white house. I walk up to it, knock, and enter. A woman is painting at an easel. She has a grotesque face, almost deformed. She points to her painting and asks if I like her self-portrait. I turn to look at it and see the most beautiful woman.

"You see and, most important, know your own beauty. It is not important how others see you if you know yourself and your inner beauty," she says.

She shows me her gallery, a long corridor with full-sized paintings. Walking along, I see each of my children.

I haven't even noticed when or how she has become the woman in the painting.

"Are you my guide?" I ask.

"I am like your eagle and camel guides," she answers. "Would you like some tea? It is like a hallucinogen, but you will be all right."

I am reluctant at first but then accept. "Does it always work?"

"It doesn't always work, you have to believe," she says.

I find myself in a huge prism with hundreds of small images of people: a little girl with a hat picking daisies, a Roman centurion, a rider on a horse, and many more. I ask if I am all of these people.

"Many directly, but you are a bit of all of them."

I am walking along a "prism" pathway. I enter a rectangular prism room where the images are much larger so that, when I look at one wall, I see only the hooves of a white horse. I'm not sure if I am inventing this, but I face the opposite wall and slowly open my eyes. There again, I see the hooves, legs, and body of a white horse. This time, I am riding it. I am wearing white armor.

I walk through another door into a beautiful garden with fountains all around, like a garden in a palace or castle. While I am admiring the beauty, I hear crying. I run along the maze of paths to find a little girl sitting beside a rose bush, holding her finger. While I can't really distinguish her face, I know that it is I.

I kneel down and say, "What is the matter?"

"The thorn from the rosebush pricked my finger."

"Why did you choose the rose when all of the other beautiful flowers have no thorns?" I ask.

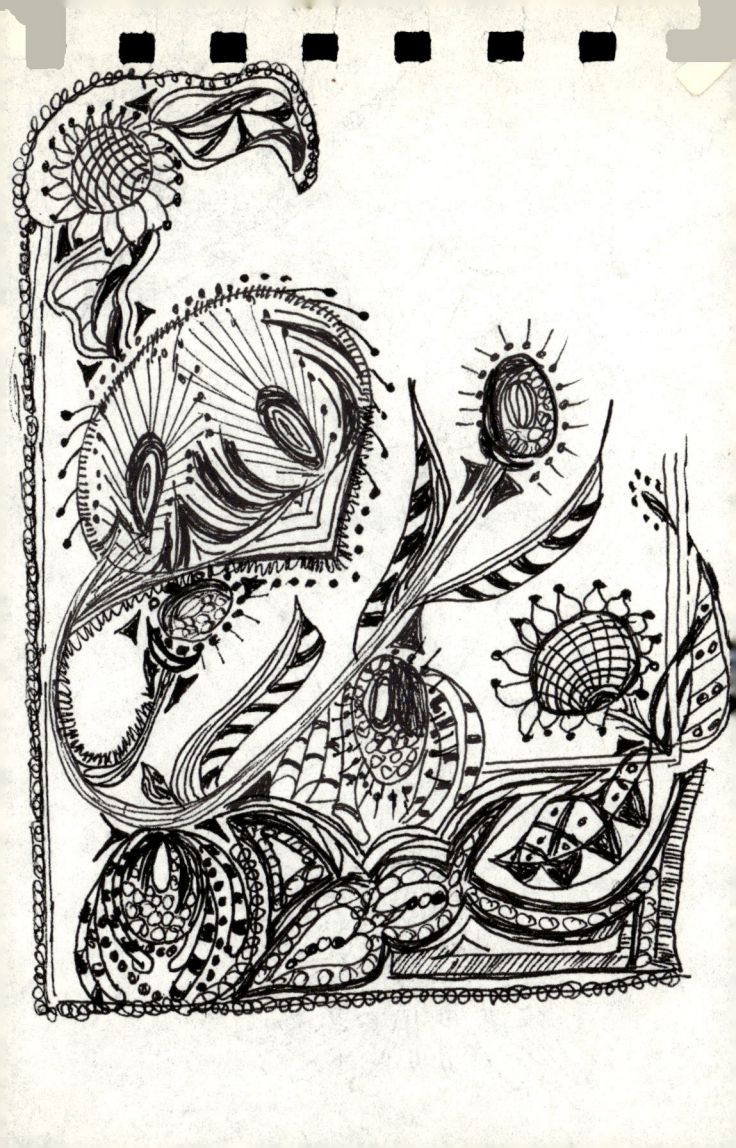

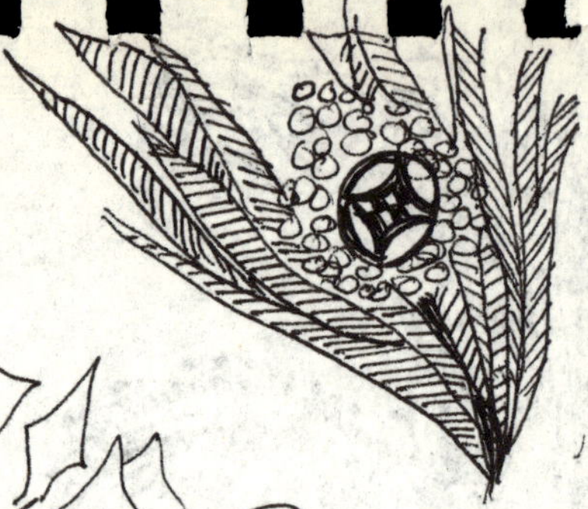

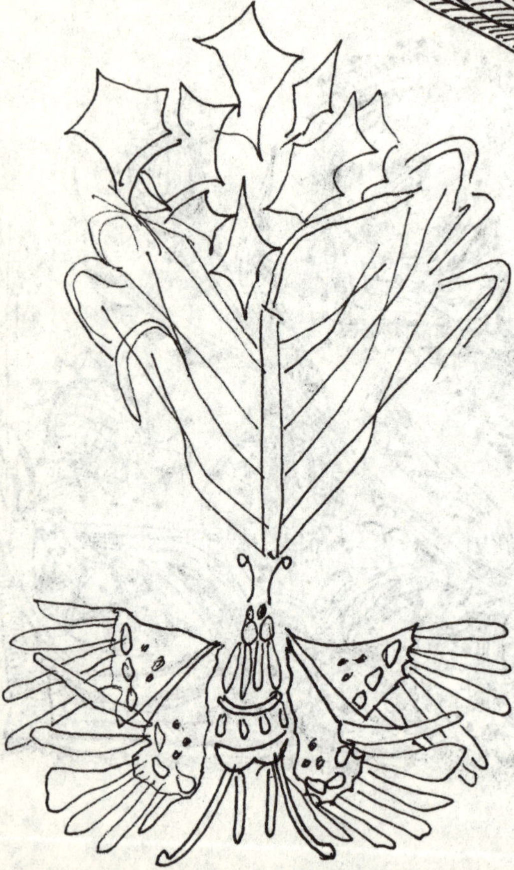

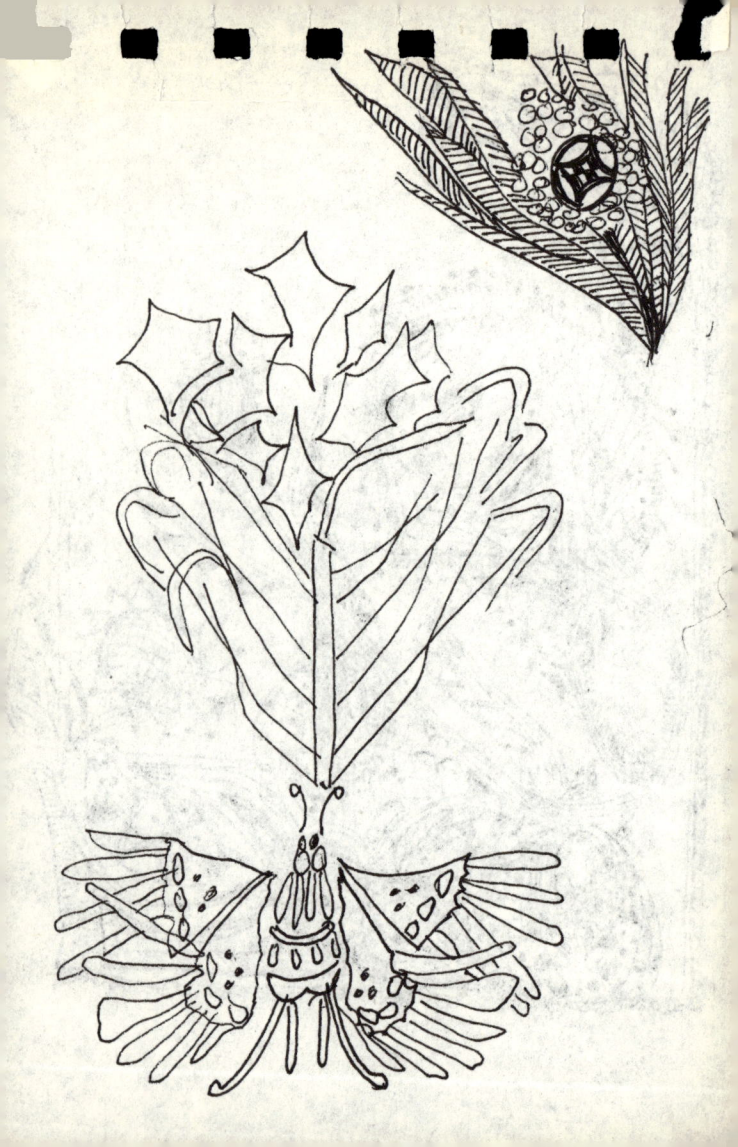

"The rose is the most beautiful flower, and I wanted it," she replies.

The woman from the white house says, "Delicate things set up barriers to protect themselves. But if that barrier becomes too thick or solid, goodness cannot enter or leave—and the barrier becomes harmful. Such is the case with the rose's thorns and the rider's armor."

She looks at each of us and says, "You need to get rid of your thorns and your armor."

I am back in the white house drinking my tea. I say my good-byes and walk back along the beach. I am so warm.

Then I can't walk, but I am not in any pain. I have to lie down on the sand with my legs bent in a fetal position. After some time, I get up and walk back along the beach to the white house. I enter and, this time, see a man painting at the easel. As before, when he turns around, he is not attractive, but his self-portrait is beautiful. We walk over to a sunroom and gaze out over a beautiful valley. He asks if I want to go to the monastery.

I say yes. I am at the monastery with all the monks milling around. Two monks, carrying a wooden bowl, come up to me.

"You need your soup," they say.

I thank them, and the three of us set off into the monastery's ground floor. They place the soup on the table for me and sit on either side. I take a spoonful and feel energy enter me. I take in a deep breath, the biggest of my life. It is amazing. When I finish, I meet my guide outside, and we wander over to the bench.

"It is so beautiful," he says.

I look upon the mountains, the clouds, and the valley with wonder and excitement. It is beautiful as always, and it never changes in its ability to soften the soul. It is all wonderful.

My Interpretation

A relaxation massage takes me to the traditional portrayal of "heaven" with angels and harps. When my Reiki treatment begins, the road remains the same, but the setting changes from heaven to earth. I feel the earth tremble. This transition from heaven to earth (Spirit to body) creates an "earthquake" with all the danger and fear associated with it—the feeling of being unsettled, off balance, not in control. My guide comforts me, saying I am feeling the energy of the earth. Nothing has changed—everything is as it always has been and always will be. There is nothing to fear.

I encounter three physical sensations in this meditation—my eyes are dry and irritated; my neck is very painful; my arm and head detach from my body.

My eyes are often an issue when I am trying to meditate. My ego is reluctant to give up its control of my sight. Yet in order to grow, I must see with vision and not sight. My guide wants me to try to see with the vision of my third eye—not because he will not help me, but to begin to teach me that I am able to do so myself. But I cannot yet. He places his hands on my eyes, and the discomfort abates—yet I only *see* his eyes, I cannot see *into* his eyes. It is only when I close my eyes and open my third eye that I see Spirit—through the connectedness of the eyes of the eagle and my guide.

Once again, I experience significant pain in my neck when my Reiki Master brings energy into my fifth chakra, the throat chakra—the energy center for communication, for truth. I have been hearing and speaking my ego's truth, thinking that I am in control of everything in my life. It is this belief that causes me such pain. I am told that I must find out why I am blocked—what issues I am holding on to that have become part of this ego belief network.

In *You Can Heal Your Life,* Louise Hay suggests, "[the neck] represents flexibility. The ability to see what's back there" (Hay, 1984, 206). Further, "[*the throat is our*] avenue of expression. Channel of creativity"

(Hay, 1984, 218). I need to look back into my past to see my blocks and recapture my creativity and my Voice.

My final physical sensation is feeling detached from my arm and head after my guide touches me. Through his touch, I am able to feel and see that I am not my body. During this time, my Reiki Master is at my root chakra. Here is the energy of group beliefs—our societal culture, our religious culture, and our family culture. I need to see all of these ingrained beliefs with the eyes of vision—see them not with judgment but with understanding—so I can heal any issues I face.

When I can see with vision, follow the Will of God, and understand that I am not my body, I am ready to learn my lessons from my next guides—the two riders, the woman and the man painting their Self-portraits. I am in my crown chakra, where everything is white—white beach, white house, white horse, and white armor. I am shown how seeing with vision is manifested in life. It begins by painting our Self-portrait of Who we truly are—Divine Beings. It is our belief in our self-worth that we project toward others. We need to paint our Self-portrait while knowing our true Inner Beauty—and *become* that portrait for others to see. When we can see our own Divine Nature, we see this same Divine Nature in everyone else.

When we see with the eyes of the ego—the eyes that believe we are separate—we see everything as out of kilter. When I enter the house, I see a deformed, grotesque face. And what we "see" with our ego is not confined to appearances; it includes what we see in others as unattractive behaviors, attitudes, and beliefs. It is not that we need condone or accept the things that we feel are unjust or wrong, but that we see the Divine Essence of that person beyond what our eyes can register. I am only seeing the woman with my eyes until she shows me her Self-portrait. This is so important for us—to paint our own picture of Self-Love and Divine Essence as well as seeing the portrait of Love in others.

This is my introduction to having tea with my guides. I will often be served tea with various guides in the future. The beautiful woman tells me it is a hallucinogen that will help me see with vision. It brings me to a prism, an object that reflects many facets of ourselves, both past and present. I am shown how I am currently wearing a full suit of armor, an impenetrable barrier to intimate connection with anyone.

As a child, I am drawn to the rose, a symbol of love—the most beautiful flower in the garden. I am that beautiful symbol of love, but I believe I need protection. The woman tells my child and me that delicate things need protection. When we are in our ego mind, we believe that we are delicate, vulnerable to threats in all that our separation entails and, therefore, in need of protection. Our Self, with all the beauty of the rose, knows that there is no scarcity, no threat. It knows that it is not delicate, as in fragile or weak, but rather intricately beautiful and infinitely powerful, with strength beyond what we can imagine. I am to remove my self-defense barriers; I do not need them; moreover, they are harmful to me. I need to become naked and vulnerable in order to expose the Divine Essence of Who I truly am.

After finishing my tea, I leave the woman, but I am unable to move. I am reborn again so that I re-enter the white house of my crown chakra to see a man painting his Self-portrait. Again, his radiance shines forth, and we spend time observing and being part of beauty. He directs me back to the monastery where I am served a bowl of soup that nourishes my body and my Soul with the biggest inbreath of Spirit of my life. I am infused with God.

How Can We Bring This into Our Lives?

Embarking on an inward journey of awareness may initially be painful. If we see this as the cleansing that it is, we will be better able to remain steadfast in our quest for Inner Peace. We need to look at what we have hidden—what keeps us captive to low self-esteem and self-worth—so that we see it with the eyes of vision and diminish its force over us.

We need to paint our Self-portrait with a brush that knows our Inner Beauty. How have we drawn our portrait? This will reflect how we will draw the portraits of others. If these portraits resemble anything but our magnificent Inner Beauty, then they are being colored by the paint of the ego, which would have us think that we are not good enough in countless ways. We need to stare at the blank page before us with the willingness and conviction that what we begin to draw with vision will be our True Self. When we can see our Self-portrait as such, we will see it in others—even if they are, as yet, unable to paint it themselves.

Most of us are wearing armor or building barriers to protect ourselves. But these things are only protecting our bodies; our Soul needs no protection since it will never be harmed by anything of this world. When we drop the barriers, we become vulnerable, not to potential threat, but to exposing our Self. In doing so, we become "safer" than we ever imagined.

Wanted

∞

February 13, 2002

I have a back and neck massage before my treatment. My Reiki Master has new music, which starts with a solo flute.

> I see the flutist on a grassy hill. Just as with the Pied Piper, I follow him as he climbs up and over the hill. At the crest of the next hill, he is joined by a number of other flutists. I follow, and I see a city below. As I descend the hill, the musicians rise into the sky and fill the air with beautiful music.
>
> I enter the city, but I don't appear to be noticed or be noteworthy. There seems to be paupers, wealthy people, and kings riding in carriages.
>
> I wander around aimlessly for a while until I see a paper on the ground with the word "Wanted" written on it. I wonder if there is a criminal around or whether

it is a job offer. I pick it up and read that it is a want ad for a waitress in a small café right in front of me.

I go inside and get the job. My uniform is a mid-thigh length, light gray dress, and a white apron with a bodice and frills around the bottom. The café has metal tables with red tops and a counter with metal stools and red seats.

Most people just want coffee. Some say it is the best coffee they've ever tasted, which amazes me because each pot sits around for ages. Two movie stars come in together and order coffee.

"Do we know you?" they ask. "You look familiar."

"I don't think so, but I certainly recognize you," I say.

"Who are you?" they ask. I start to answer the typical responses of what I am like, what I do, but I can't. What do those responses mean? *Who am I?* I don't know the answer.

I carry on waitressing, trying to answer the question.

The actors say, "We have to leave now and go back to our other world, but we will try to come in every day to answer the question for ourselves and find a higher peace."

My boss says that it is time for my coffee break. I try to leave through the front door, but it is locked. I go to the small, dark room at the back.

My Reiki Master is at my throat chakra.

Once again, I have pain and feel like my head is turning—but not as badly as before. My guide comes into the room.

"How am I going to get out of the café if I can't answer the question 'Who am I'?" I ask.

"I will return and take you out the back way if you are having trouble," he answers.

My Reiki Master moves from my throat.

My coffee break is over, and I go back to waitressing in the light again. A street person and a successful writer come in at the same time. They sit at the counter and say that each is also the other.

I continue to be plagued by the question—Who am I? Then someone opens a door in the wall that I had never seen. A bright light shines through the doorway. There is a great cheer in the café; everyone applauds this person's transition from this world into a new realm of Spirit. This is the goal of everyone in the café. Most of the customers come and go through the front door. They have not reached the level to exit through this "hidden" door.

When someone leaves through the front door, I look outside and see a lineup of people anxiously waiting to get inside. One customer asks how I got the job and says how lucky I am to be able to stay inside all the time and work. I feel a little guilty that I cannot answer the question "Who am I?"; maybe I am not working hard enough.

After what seems to be days of waitressing and serving coffee (and stale coffee at that) I leave through the hidden door in the wall. I am in a big field. I sit down and then leave my body. I can still see myself sitting on the grass. I am drawn skyward, quickly passing clouds, into the atmosphere until I am in the calm, gravity-free universe. I am just floating around. I think that it will be quiet, but I can hear the music. I stay for some time, still able to see the earth and myself on the ground. Eventually, I come back to earth and to my body, but unlike leaving my body very quickly, on the way down, I float gently through every layer.

I go to the monastery and sit on the bench with my guide. I kneel down to look at the flower that my grandfather carved. My guide tells me that my grandfather carved just one small petal of the flower, but thousands of people helped finish the carving. He shows me where I have started to carve a small petal on the edge of the bench, just as the upright part of the chair curves around to the top. There are small etchings or scratches in the stone. He tells me that I am just beginning to make my flower.

"I am frustrated by not knowing Who I am," I say. He leads me to a small room with a glowing crystal in the middle.

"Look deeply inside it," he says.

I see myself as a baby and then as a child. But what does this mean? I still do not understand. We go outside.

"You are the wind, the rainbow, the rock, the trees—you are everything," he says. "You are part of the Universe, and the Universe is part of you. Everyone and everything is special and important."

He knows I have to go, and he gives me a big hug.

"I have so much to teach you. Come back soon," he says.

My Interpretation

The Pied Piper leads me to a town where, unlike every other town I have entered, I am not noticed and do not appear noteworthy. Despite outward appearances, everyone seems to be viewed the same. The town encompasses all economic levels, all races, all nationalities, all abilities, all mental states—everyone—regardless of how society sees them. Everyone who comes to the café is equally valued.

When I enter this town, I see a "Wanted" sign and think of two possibilities—one fear-based and the other opportunity-based. Do we bypass the opportunity to enter the café because of fear? Do we make the effort to pick up on the sign before us? I am wanted as a waitress in a diner of the 1950s (the decade of my birth), complete with vintage uniform. I have come into the café through a different route than the others. I have been "sent" to this place for my learning.

What is this café? It is the metaphorical place that we enter when we still our mind, calm our bodies, and let go of the 60,000 thoughts that inhabit, and inhibit, our brain. It is meditation, it is calming exercises—it is being present in the moment. When we are here, we drink the best coffee we have ever tasted—we "drink in" our True Self, our Divine Essence. The coffee never changes, and I presume that it is stale. But God never changes; He is changeless, Eternal, Infinite.

Those who want to enter the café do so and stay as long as they wish. Those who are waiting in line *wish* to "get in," realizing it is a desirable, helpful place. But the endless stream of thoughts, the to-do lists, and the difficulty focusing keep them from reaching the door. However, the more we persevere, the closer we will get to that front door.

Everyone comes into the café to find the answer to "Who am I?" Two actors pose the question to me. Actors—people playing someone they are not. When we believe we are not our Divine Self, we are actors playing a role as separate bodies. The role will end—as all roles do—but most often, we do not even know that we are acting.

I begin to answer the question from my self (my ego), but I know that this is not Who I am, and I do not, cannot, respond. But I do not yet know the Truth of Who I am. I am rendered speechless. I find it so difficult and sad that I have no answer. I have stilled my ego, but I have not heard my Spirit.

I am given a break. I temporarily leave my connection with Spirit and experience the fight of my ego in the darkness of the back room when my neck feels like it is being ripped off (although less than before). The struggle is painful, but my guide tells me he will return and help me, if need be. I will always have help, but I also need to know that I *can* get out myself.

I do not understand anything about this place. I do not understand why everyone wants to be here. Why do they stand outside in long lines waiting to get in? Why do they think the old coffee is the best they have ever had? The patrons are the ones who tell me how good it feels to be here. They ask me the question I am to answer; they know about the portal in the wall and are excited when someone passes through it. Everyone inside knows the question—and struggles to answer it. When it is time to go, most leave through the front door and return to the outside world, albeit with a great sense of peace. I am unable to leave; it is my "job" to stay in this place of calm mind long enough to absorb its Truth.

Eventually, I have stayed in the café long enough to become centered, focused, and open to my Divine within. I can now exit through the opening in the wall, and I find myself in a field. I leave my body, rapidly being pulled up, magnetized to my Higher Self, no longer a body. I *experience* the Universe. When I return to my body, I float down slowly; this gentle transition allows me to be *in* my body but not *of* it.

Although I have *experienced* Who I am, I have not *internalized* it. I still cannot answer Who am I?—I have not been able to connect my "five-senses" experience floating in the universe with my *being* part of the Universe.

At the monastery, my guide provides this connection. He brings me to an all-knowing crystal ball. Not only is it a crystal ball but a glowing crystal ball; Eternal Light illuminates from it. I see myself as an infant and a child inside it, yet still I do not understand. My guide tells me that I am Everything. I am part of the Universe, and the Universe is part of me.

How Do We Bring This into Our Lives?

The café is symbolically the "antechamber" before *being* One with the Universe, One with all that we are as Divine Beings. It is that place of meditation—in whatever form that means to us. It is where we want to be, where we constantly want to return. Sometimes we may feel we are always just lining up to get in—we cannot focus or feel anything. *When is our time? Why do others keep getting in? Will I ever get through?* This is the ego trying to thwart our plans. If we try so hard to fight back, the ego will just be strengthened. The practice and vigilance of "lining up" will eventually get us through the door. Then our next time in the "lineup" will be much shorter.

But sometimes we are hesitant to even line up for the café. We do not like change, we do not like the unknown, the notion of looking backwards in order to change the path we are headed on. If we find ourselves feeling this way, it is all the more reason for us to at least stand at the back of the line and listen to those coming out as they pass by.

When we have stayed in the "café" long enough to detach from our ego by drinking in our radiance, the opening appears for us to experience our Self. That opening may be a vision, a greater sense of peace, a feeling of being overwhelmed with bliss, a miracle, or a "knowing." It can be anything that fills our Soul.

Entering the café is an important start to awareness of our Self. We come in the front door of the café from the world of ego and leave through the side door into the world of Spirit.

How do we answer: "Who am I?" Do we answer with the Voice of our Self or the voice of our self? Do we see ourselves as Divine or do we define ourselves by what we do, what we have—measurements of this world.

Who am I? I am the Universe. I am Everything.

Cleansed of My Gold

∞

February 27, 2002

I am having a Reiki treatment.

> I immediately find myself in a jungle. I sit down and marvel at the light filtering through the huge leaves. Eventually, I hear water running, and I find myself at the edge of a murky river. A raft has just floated by with a group of people on it. The steersman keeps looking back at me. I can see the whites of his eyes so well against the blackness of his skin. I wonder what dangers lurk ahead for them, particularly hippos.
>
> Another raft comes drifting by, but this one stops right in front of me. There are three other people on the raft. Finally, the steersman holds out his hand. I hesitate but eventually climb aboard.

The jungle is very peaceful. I expected that it would be noisy. We pass under a canopy of tree limbs used by monkeys as a bridge across the water. Muted light filters down to us.

Soon we float to shore and start to walk. We come upon a most beautiful waterfall. It is not too wide and has a magnificent canyon shaped like a horseshoe. It brings tears to my eyes, and I think, *This is God's beauty*. I am awestruck and stand motionless for some time.

I lie on my stomach and look over the edge of the cliff to the valley floor. It is so deep. The top of the waterfall is right beside me. I turn around to the steersman, and we exchange smiles. All I can see are beautiful white teeth. I stand up, and we hug; both of us lie down and gaze into the valley and around the canyon walls.

Soon an eagle lands beside me. I put my hand on his back and gently pat his feathers. I move to his chest and feel all of his feathers. When I touch his head, I realize he is a golden eagle, not a bald eagle. He opens his beak, and I touch his tongue. I look into his eye and see my distorted reflection, as if I were looking in a convex mirror.

I ask if he is going to fly me around. He slowly lifts his talon for me to touch. I feel its strength and sharpness. He carefully steps onto my back and gently grips his talons into my gray sweatshirt. We begin to soar around, and I wonder for a moment if I am going to be sick from the motion.

The eagle finds a break in the wall, like a cave, behind the waterfall. We fly in there and rest, looking out at the valley walls from behind the waterfall. The view is blurry.

From there, we fly along the wall, arriving at nests of cliff swallows. We fly close to them, and I can see their nests in the holes of the sandy cliff wall. They don't seem to notice or be bothered by us.

Further along, we come to a jungle area where monkeys are swinging from tree to tree and jungle birds are flying about. We fly across the valley and duck into a crevasse I had not noticed before. There is another beautiful waterfall with a pool at the bottom. A naked man, woman, and baby are bathing in the pool. They are having such fun and seem to be very much of a family.

After they get out, an old woman, naked as well, enters the water. She relaxes and smiles in the pool. An old man joins her. I then realize that this must be a baptism. I look along the wall and see that the line for the pool is kilometers long.

It is my turn. I am so hesitant. Does this mean I would be committing to Christianity? I dip my toe in and out a number of times, worried and frightened to commit. But then I see a priest, a Buddhist, a Jew, a Sikh, a Muslim, and a Hindu on the far bank. They all bid me come into the water.

I enter willingly, and the water all around me becomes gold. It feels wonderful. Then I notice little flutterings on top of the water. I immerse myself up to my neck and realize they are fairies—hundreds of them. They are all dancing and playing. Behind me, a fairy who is dressed as the devil is hitting everyone and creating havoc. I try to turn away but realize I must watch this scene. I stare at the devil and, eventually, he takes off his horns and his cape and mixes with the other fairies. He is happy.

One of the smaller fairies puts on the horns, but they are too big. So he puts them down. The other fairies stomp on the devil's clothes until the cape and horns disappear under the water.

Gold fairy dust sprinkles down from above as all the ferries disappear. I stand up and watch the gold water rippling down and away from my waist.

I walk to the other side and the priest, the Jew, the Sikh, the Muslim, the Buddhist, and the Hindu all give me a hand out. My legs and arms feel very light, like I am levitating, but my head feels like it is on solid ground.

I feel incredible. The eagle flies my clothes over, and we take off again. I thank him for taking me there; although he doesn't answer in words, I can hear his reply, "You're welcome."

He takes me to the top of a huge tree and leaves me on a branch where there are boa constrictors and huge baboons. The snakes are raising their heads and hissing; the baboons are fighting terribly, falling among the branches. My neck and the back of my head start to hurt, and I feel my head turn to the right so that it is parallel to the ground.

I keep saying to myself that the eagle wouldn't have left me here if it was not safe. But I am scared, and I hate to hear all the fighting.

Eventually, dawn starts to filter through the tree, and my fears start to subside. I am able to stand up; I decide that I need to move, but do I go up the branch to the light (and supposed safety) or toward the tree trunk and darkness? I decide to make my way along the tree limbs to the trunk. To my amazement, there is a chair carved into the big limb. I sit and feel calm. The pain at the base of my skull rises up my head and out the top.

My eagle comes and says I am all right. He flies me across the valley until I see what looks like a small babbling brook. As I approach, I realize it is a spring, changing from hot to cold. I bathe in its warm pool below.

I journey to the center of the earth to find the origin of this spring. I feel like I am in a fetal position in a womb. I hear someone say that I am getting ready to be reborn.

I look around and realize that all of the millions of specks of sand are adults in wombs, preparing to be reborn.

"I'm not sure if I am ready," I say.

"If you are down here and can see yourself in the womb, then you are ready," someone responds.

I push, kick, and hammer my way out of the womb and float peacefully up to the surface. Once there, I have a cool drink from the spring.

The eagle arrives, and we talk about what has happened. He sits on my shoulder as we walk out of the forest toward the light. We are in a large deciduous forest with so little undergrowth that the forest has a clean, clear, open look. We make it out of the forest and into the sunlight.

I study a map for some time before deciding on a path to the left. I take off on my new pathway with my eagle on my shoulder.

He says, "You've picked the right road."

I am so happy that I lift my arms; immediately, hundreds of butterflies and small birds land on my arms and all over my head.

My Interpretation

I *expect* the jungle to be unsafe; I expect danger and hippos, even though it is not frightening at the time. We are so often fearful of any number of negative outcomes. My ego fears are lost when I stay in the present and marvel at the Divine Light filtering down.

The boat that is to take me and others "somewhere" floats calmly to shore. I am hesitant to board, frightened of potential danger. However, when nothing happens, I become calm. I am calm in this world when I do not fear danger, when I understand that I will be safe.

Our destination is the waterfalls, which appear to be the spectacular Victoria Falls. They bring tears to my eyes, and I see them as God's beauty. When we feel this "fireworks of joy" within us, we are connected with our Divine Essence. The spark may be a beautiful sunset, spectacular scenery, a newborn baby, or a loved one. Sometimes we see the spark as something outside of us, and we dismiss it as temporary or unrelated to us specifically. But these feelings are markers—the physical, emotional, mental, and spiritual clues and signs of our way to our Self. They are what being connected to our Self *feels* like.

After I have felt every part of my eagle guide, and I see myself in him, he flies me to my lesson. But during the flight, I feel motion sickness. When we take this leap, things can become so disjointed from our current beliefs, thoughts, and experiences that we can feel off balance. We need to stay with the journey; our discomfort will pass.

My eagle flies me to a cave behind the waterfalls, and I observe this world through a filter; everything looks blurry. I am learning to see with vision. I then am taken to a crevasse that I could not previously see but has always been there; I am seeing with greater awareness.

I quickly realize that I am at a baptismal waters and anxiety overtakes me. I equate baptism with Christianity. At this point, I fear that, if I travel the path of Christianity, I will lose Who I am; I will lose my Self in the rituals; I must return to the belief in a fearful God; the only way to Him is through the church. What I really fear is fundamentalism (which exists in many of the religious paths), but my only exposure to religion is Christianity. When I see the unity of the religions—and that the baptism is a universal cleaning and connection to the Divine—I feel comfortable with entering the baptismal waters of Oneness. There, I am cleansed of my gold skin, my attachment to this ego world (see "The City of Gold").

All of the gold (my ego thoughts of who I am, that I have not been touched by love) falls easily from my body and mind in this water. Believing that I am a body—that I am my ego, a separate self—does not make me a bad person. Most of my fairies are playing and dancing, but that one "devil" (the ego representative) behind me creates the disconnect with my Soul and the constant battering of my "good" fairies. It is only when I look at my ego without fear, without ignoring it, that it relinquishes its hold on me. Another fairy tries to take over, but the horns are too heavy in this cleansing pool—they carry such a debilitating weight. In these waters, the fairies can collectively drown the horns and cape of the ego. We must remain vigilant and examine our ego without compromise—and without judgment—for it has a strong foothold on us.

After being cleansed of my ego-gold to be the Love that I am, I am being led to trust. During the dark night, I face many fears represented by the dangerous animals. I experience the same pains in my fifth chakra, the throat chakra, as my ego fights to keep control. But I am able to tell myself that I am safe here; my guides have led me to this place. I am following the Will of God. I trust that this is exactly where I am to be—and that I am completely safe. When I see the light at the end of this dark night and am able to calm myself, the pain rises from my body. My Will is no longer with my ego self but with my Self, and my eagle guide takes me to be reborn. What does it mean to be reborn? It means letting go of the past, and with it, recapturing my understanding of Who I am. It is with this rebirth that I am now on the correct path, and my Essence attracts the birds and butterflies.

How Do We Bring This into Our Lives?

"It's a jungle out there" is an expression often used for the "survival-of-the-fittest" mentality of our world. If we *expect* danger to be lurking around every bend, then we will never take the journey that is intended for us. Fear of the future is based on experiences of the past—either ours or another's. The past is the domain of the ego. The path determined by our Higher Self does not include the past. If the path we are currently on is entrenched in our past and it does not serve us, we need to change that path—and change it with Divine Guidance.

When we feel that explosion of serenity in our heart, we need to remember the feeling and know it is the sensation of Who we are, a reflection of our Divine Being.

By getting on the "boat" meant for us, we are taken to exactly the learning for us. The symbolic baptismal waters cleanse me of my ego attachment. These waters are not specific to any one religion, and they do not exclude any path. Whichever path resonates with us and holds true to our Higher Self will cleanse us of our belief that we are our bodies. We need to enter that mystical pool of water—not to be better humanitarians (we generally are this already)—but to be our Self, and exude the resulting peace, joy, and love for others to embrace.

My Eagle's Spirit Breath

∞

MARCH 20, 2002

We have just come home from a family ski trip. Before Reiki, I have a massage, which feels great. Flutes are playing in the music.

> I am sitting in a meadow with my arms around my knees. The piper is standing right beside me. Another piper is playing on a far hill. The music echoes back and forth. More pipers join in, and their music surrounds me.
>
> I then have a strong sense of jealousy about "sharing" my friends.
>
> "What is this jealousy?" I ask.
>
> My guide explains, "You are a blade of grass, and all your best friends are beside you. Your roots intertwine. But each of these friends has their closest friends around them with their roots intertwined. If you do not have a circle of friends/family, then you will lean too much on

one person, and they will be pushed over. You need to know that love in friendship and family is not singular, but divisible among all who need and share it."

My Reiki Master is at my throat chakra.

I have a different sensation in my neck today. Other times, my head pulls to the right and is quite painful. Now it pulls to the left and is not sore at all. It feels quite light actually. Then I feel as if my neck is extended up and my head is tilted completely back. An eagle picks me up by my neck with his beak, not his talons, and flies me across the land. I feel light and am suspended only by my neck. He eventually puts me down on the top of a mountain.

"I can talk," I exclaim with delight. "I can speak." I am so happy.

I am alone until an old man comes around the corner. I think I should talk with him. Maybe I do, but I keep falling in and out of sleep. I remember going around to the back of the mountain where it is dark. I am skiing on this dark backside and am frightened because I don't know where to go or how. Eventually, someone guides me to a glimmer of light.

My Interpretation

Jealousy prompts the lesson that love is completely and infinitely divisible—that to lean on any one person, or to wish or need their love or attention conditionally, creates instability and co-dependency.

This is the fifth meditation where my neck is twisted, and the first where I do not experience considerable pain (see "The City of Gold," "Painting our Self-Portrait," "Wanted," and "Cleansed of My Gold"). Today, my head and neck are being pulled in the opposite direction; for the first time, my eagle can carry me in his beak, not his talons. He breathes Spirit directly into me and opens my throat chakra. Now I have my Voice—at least the intellectual understanding of it—and I delight and rejoice in this. However, I do not use my newfound Voice. I am not yet sure what It wants to say, what It sounds like.

There is still a dark mountain I need to explore—but there is a light and someone there to guide me.

How Do We Bring This into Our Lives?

It can be so easy, so tempting, to lean on any one of our friends or family—and this not only relates to using them as a sounding board but also to needing them to enhance our life. There is nothing wrong with best friends or family members—far from it—but if an unhealthy dependency develops, our roots may end up choking each other.

Our upbringing, with the best of intentions, guides us to what we "should" say, how we "should" feel. We may struggle with finding our Voice even when we have unblocked this chakra. Unblocking it may be the first step; the next steps are discovering what our Voice needs and wants to say.

Teachings of the Dogwood

∞

March 27, 2002

At my Reiki treatment this morning, I immediately fall into a deep meditation.

> I am in a meadow with the grasses blowing gently in the wind. There is a piper beside me, with several others echoing back from distant hilltops. The piper indicates that I should follow him along a narrow, sandy, worn path leading to the monastery.
>
> The piper leaves me there, and I walk through the gate to meet my guide.
>
> "Hello. I have not been here in a long time. I have had so much on my mind," I say.
>
> "I understand, but you should still come," he says.
>
> We walk through the most beautiful gardens.

"Do you know the flowers that are covering the ground all around us?" he asks.

"Yes, they're dogwoods," I answer.

"Do you know what they mean?" he asks.

"Yes. The yellow center is the energy, and the four petals are love, joy, peace, and happiness," I answer.

"These result from the true meaning, but they are not the meaning," he says. "The first is awareness, then unity, then universe, and finally understanding. With these petals intact and spun around in a circle, all will be perfect for the love, joy, peace, and happiness you described. The central yellow is energy, but it is the physical energy for life, energy needed for survival, and not necessarily the spiritual life force.

"Beauty and perfection are in what is common, not in the unique. What is common and everyday will lead us to understanding the Truth. The unique is magnificent, but the fundamentals of Truth can sometimes get lost. A rose is beautiful, but it takes a good deal of attention and extra care. The dogwoods grow freely and uninhibited wherever they can. Look for the common.

"The garden starts as an open area. Nature alone determines what is going to be there and where it is going to be located within it."

The garden is so beautiful, so magnificent.

We move into the monastery.

"It doesn't look like a typical Buddhist monastery," I say. "It has a ceiling like the Sistine Chapel, columns like the Parthenon, and mats for Muslims—something for most religions."

"That is correct because all religions ultimately offer the same teachings," he explains. "Consider an old wagon wheel with metal spokes and a wooden rim. At the end of each spoke is a religion. The truly-learned masters of each religion are moving down their spokes to the hub. Many of them are near it. But less-learned leaders are slow and hesitant to move, out of fear and lack of knowledge. They do not see the similarities when you take away all the dogma and man-made rules. But mankind will get there and is moving in the right direction," he says.

A group of "modern" monks comes in. One female touches me on the shoulder and nods in welcome. Then she takes me aside, and we link arms back to back. Eventually, I can see not only ahead of me but also behind me, through her. Two others join, and I can see in four directions. Then a group joins, and I can see the whole 360 degrees, although the backside is a bit foggy. The others leave, and the female monk and I again link arms together. I can see behind me clearly.

I see a yellow butterfly through the window dancing to the music. I put my arm out the window, and he lands on it. I bring it inside and start dancing to the music. Hundreds of yellow butterflies land on my head, my arms, and my torso. When I twirl, they all rise up and flutter in a circular motion above my head, and alight when I stop twirling.

Eventually, my guide joins me, bringing his black butterflies. When we twirl, all the butterflies mingle. More and more monks join in, each bringing their own butterflies: purple, red, green, blue. The butterflies swirl around our heads in an incredible display.

One by one, the monks leave with their butterflies. My guide leaves last. I dance for a while longer and then kneel on one knee. Only one butterfly remains. I take the butterfly back to the window, and it flies off.

My guide and I walk outside to the bench. A large branch of a nearby tree acts like an umbrella. I am amazed that I haven't noticed it before.

"It helps you to see because, without it, you have to squint in the sunlight. What do you see today?" he asks.

As usual, I see a beautiful mountain, but I also see something shining. My guide hands me binoculars. I see that it is something man-made.

"Oh, it's only man-made," I say, disappointed.

"That doesn't matter," he says. "You can learn from man as well as from nature."

I get up to cross the great chasm to this beautiful vista. I know there are bridges. I can't see them yet, but I know I will be safe. I realize this is what faith is; my physical senses are telling me not to step out into the huge void, but my spiritual mind tells me there are bridges.

We walk along a bridge, and I realize that this is so much like flying. There is nothing ahead, behind, or for kilometers below. I see a man playing a harp on a bridge to the left. A bald eagle is perched on his head. The eagle flies over, picks us up and carries us to the mountains. All I hear is the sound of his powerful wings in flight.

I see the shining object: a small, silver box with jewels on the top and sides. Inside is beautiful notepaper bound in ribbons. They are love letters, and underneath is a locket. Inside are two pictures, a man and a woman from the 1930s. Then they change to Egyptians from centuries ago, then modern Asians, and then back to Anglo-Saxons.

While coming back along the bridge, I am awestruck at the beauty before me. The monastery is perched on a sheer cliff with waterfalls streaming down.

"How did you know which path to take to the mountains?" my guide asks.

"I thought they all went there," I say.

"No, they don't." He turns on a switch to show all the bridges. Only one of hundreds goes to the mountains.

We make our way to a calming meadow on the left. Canada geese are all about. I pet one of them, and a number come over and kiss me with their beaks. When a large snake starts crawling up my arm and coils itself on my head, I am afraid.

My guide says, "This is fear. Just work through it."

I concentrate on being safe. Eventually, the snake slithers down to position itself in front of my face. It then lifts its head and nods good-bye.

We go back to the monastery, and my guide tells me that I am going through a dimensional shift.

"What do you mean?" I say.

"There are many dimensions to our plane, mostly spiritual. You are shifting your beliefs such that you are moving toward your spiritual body."

My Interpretation

The monastery grounds provide important lessons in this meditation. My guide and I walk through the most beautiful gardens, with most of the groundcover being low-lying, four-leafed white flowers. (I have always known these plants as dogwoods, but they are actually bunchberries of the dogwood family.) When I am asked what they mean, I confidently answer love, joy, peace, and happiness—the *results* of living in Spirit. But it is *through* the teachings of the petals of the dogwood flower that we are connected with these powerful, positive emotions we so desire.

I am taught the meaning of the first petal (awareness, bringing love) by way of a garden. This beautiful garden is Who we are, Divine Love. It is magnificent, open, and filled with awareness of our Higher Self. In this garden of Divine Love, each plant grows as it should, where it is best suited, and blossoms in its own time. Nothing of our ego selves determines how this garden unfolds or looks—it cannot, for it does not know the Unconditional Love that we are.

The second petal (unity, bringing joy) is taught through seeing the monastery as a resplendent multi-denominational structure with aspects of many religions embedded in the building. My guide further explains unity with the metaphor of a giant wagon wheel. I will be taught more about this wheel later, but in my introduction to it, my guide teaches of religious masters and less-learned religious leaders. The former are moving down each of their respective spokes to the center, to God—however they name "All That Is". Most of them have united with Truth of their religion, which is the same universal Truth of all the other spokes. By contrast, less-learned religious leaders are fearful and focus on fundamentalist rigidity, and they see only differences between themselves and others. They are not moving toward their stated beliefs. But collectively, we are moving in the right direction toward understanding the unity of us all; with this, we are filled with joy.

I learn the teachings of the third petal (universe, bringing peace) when I lock arms with one monk and then many more. I see everything around me, beyond what my human eyesight and perspective can see, to the whole Universe, the whole of Everything. This knowledge of Universal Vision brings us Inner Peace. We are able to see from every perspective when we join with our neighbors, see through their eyes—and through their bodies to Infinity. The peace that results from this experience joins us all. There is no inner conflict; there is no external conflict.

The fourth petal (understanding, bringing happiness) is taught through the butterfly. In Native American teachings, Butterfly medicine is transformation. Sams and Carson's *Medicine Cards* says:

> Like Butterfly, you are always at a certain stage in your life activities . . . The final stage of transformation is the leaving of the chrysalis and birth. This last step involves sharing the colors and joy of your creation with the world. (Sams and Carson, 1999, 73)

This fourth petal is the completion of the transformation—the crystallization of the *understanding* of all the other petals—to an *awareness* of our Self, the *unity* or ultimate "sameness" of each of us and of our paths, and the *universe* when seeing Infinity through others' eyes. With our birth from this process, we experience true happiness.

The Native American teachings of the Medicine Wheel may be helpful in understanding the colors of our butterflies. The Medicine Wheel is a symbol for the circle of life, the concept that all lies within and around this circle. The Wheel is divided into four quadrants, with the north being white, the east yellow, south red, and west black. (Some traditions have red as east and south as yellow). The Medicine Wheel represents many aspects of our learning, including the four directions, the four races, and the four stages of life (birth, adolescence, adulthood, death). My butterflies are yellow, the color of the east, innocence, where we are born into this physical life. My guide's butterflies are black, the west, where we have spiritual insight, dreams, and visions to go within to understand our Self and to have knowledge. The other monks' colors are purple, red, green, and blue. In many Native teachings, purple is Self, red is adolescence, green is Mother Earth, and blue is Father Sky. All of our butterflies are intertwining to create perfect balance. I am beginning my journey around the Medicine Wheel.

We learn this transformation in our everyday lives. The retreats we attend, the spiritual talks we hear, and the spiritual books we read are of great help and inspiration; they often hold the beauty of the rose. If we do not bring what we felt, what we heard, and what we learned into our everyday lives, we will not move forward toward the love, joy, peace, and happiness that we so cherish. That is why the center of the flower is what sustains our everyday lives and not the spiritual energy I had originally answered in my explanation to my guide. Albert Einstein said, "The whole of science is nothing more than a refinement of everyday thinking" (Einstein, 1936, 349).

From the lessons of the dogwood, I am taken to experience faith. Faith is *knowing* we will be "taken" to exactly where we need to be—if we follow Spirit. I have always landed on exactly the right bridge to take me where my lessons await me. Others have their own bridges. In this meditation, my bridge leads me to a jeweled box full of love letters and pictures of a couple who change not only in time but in race. Love is the connection; we are all the same—not in looks or human characteristics—but in our Divine Essence. I mistakenly believe I cannot learn anything from man-made objects. Everything is a potential lesson.

I have been given the elements for *living* Oneness through the petals of the dogwood. But I am still fearful. A snake appears to me, slithers up my arm, and sits on my head. Snake medicine is transmutation. Sams and Carson's *Medicine Cards* tells us:

> The transmutation of the life-death-rebirth cycle is exemplified by the shedding of Snake's skin. It is the energy of wholeness, cosmic consciousness, and the ability to experience anything willingly and without resistance. It is the knowledge that all things are equal in creation, and that those things which might be experienced as poison can be eaten, ingested, integrated, and transmuted if one has the proper state of mind. (Sams and Carson, 1999, 61)

I am afraid to shed my skin, to change, to live differently. I have been given the information, but I am fearful to shed who I think I am—a body that lives in another world when not in meditation. While I am willing to experience anything in meditation, I have not been able to bring my visions into my life. I must learn that whatever I *think* is harmful or poisonous to me (whether consciously or unconsciously) is not—and it will not harm me. I am able to face this fear because I understand that I am to experience it for a reason. In doing so, my fear leaves; it simply disappears with acknowledgment. I have transmuted; I have shed my snake skin to go through a dimensional shift, a shift in living more in Spirit in this world.

How Do We Bring This into Our Lives?

The petals of the dogwood offer us a focus to live in Spirit. By becoming aware of our Self, we live with love. By seeing unity (Oneness) as we all stand on the same wagon wheel, we receive joy. By experiencing the universe (Infinity) through, and by, all others, we receive peace. By understanding how these all connect to become the circle of One, we receive happiness.

When we have faith in these Truths and believe that, when we follow our Inner Guidance, we will be safe, our energy changes—and we shift out of this world of illusion.

Unlocking My Soul

∞

April 3, 2002

During my Reiki treatment, the flute/piper music is playing.

> I am immediately in the same meadow with a few rolling hills. But unlike before, the musicians are not human. I first notice the high notes. I look up and see a chickadee singing beautifully and loudly. Then a dolphin, with his head out of the water, is enthusiastically singing along to another note. The lowest notes are sung by the hippo; he just seems to open his mouth and bellow. The fourth sound is made by a snake singing and swaying to the music. I watch, listen, and enjoy their concert for quite a while.
>
> I go over to the dolphin and pet him. He feels so smooth and cool, with no bumps or flaws. Then the chickadee flies over and lands on my hand. The hippo

waddles into the deep water and swims over with his mouth wide open. The snake slithers over and up my arm. The beautiful chorus is all around me.

When I know I have to leave, the chickadee flies to the top of the dolphin's head, the snake slithers up the dolphin's nose to his forehead, and the dolphin, with his riders, puts his head in the open mouth of the hippo. As I leave, I turn around to see them all so contently intertwined.

I am wearing a white T-shirt with a denim-like peasant dress and sandals. *I never dress like this.* I walk along a narrow road, at peace in the warmth of the sun. I come to a crossroads and stop to contemplate which way to go. I decide to face each of the three directions, close my eyes, and see if I can feel anything.

I turn right and do not notice a change from the warmth and comfort I felt. Facing straight ahead, my stomach starts to hurt—and I am agitated. Turning to the left, I feel uncomfortable as well. I turn back to the right, and the good feelings return. It is amazing.

I proceed along the road to the right. I come upon a very old man sitting atop a small knoll on the left. I approach him and sit down. I talk to him but he doesn't speak, he just nods. I eventually realize that he is a listening man—and he is teaching me to listen.

He says, "You are not a great listener, but you are getting better." I am not happy with myself.

Then we connect with total communication—talking and listening. He takes my head in his hands and starts to roll it slowly in a small circle and then faster in a large circle.

"Something is blocking your throat. I have to get it out," he says.

He disconnects my head from my body and starts jiggling it up and down. He works at dislodging this block for some time. Eventually, a large marble rolls out, and he reattaches my head.

"You will now be able to feel the hole. Bring air from your toes, through this opening, up to your head," he instructs. I feel the openness.

He gives me a soft leather pouch that slings over my shoulder. "Put your marble in the pouch and carry it around with you," he says.

He shows me his pouch. It is bigger and full of marbles—all different sizes—and the big ones are on the bottom. "Your throat may well block up again. You need to dislodge the marble and put it in your pouch. At first, the marbles may be big, but over time, as you recognize that a marble is forming, you can dislodge it when it is very small. Your pouch will remind you that you have to keep vigilant with this, and it will show you your progress as the marbles get smaller," he says.

"Why is your pouch bigger than mine, even though you are so learned?" I ask him.

"I didn't start as young as you are. It took me a long time. I will make you another pouch if you need it," he answers.

I bend down to thank him and kiss him good-bye.

I start to cry uncontrollably in both the meditation and on the table. Great sobs and tears ensue. I am still crying when I walk away from him, and my crying gets worse when I turn to wave good-bye. As I follow the path, I calm down, although tears keep streaming down my face on the table.

I walk further along and come upon an old woman on the right. She doesn't talk at first. It occurs to me that she is mute and that this is another lesson—to say what I want and what I mean. But what do I want to say? What do I really want sometimes?

She says, "You have to unlock your Soul and find out what is there and what you want. Everyone has a small box of keys hidden in their body. You need to get that box and unlock your organs to find out your true desires."

I crawl into my mouth and notice that my insides are flooded. Holding my breath and wearing a miner's light, I dive into the darkness. Deep down, I see a shiny, silvery box. I grab it, rush to the surface for air, crawl out my mouth, jump down to my shoulder, and run along my arm to put the box in my hand. It is blue and beautifully wrapped in silver foil with a bow. Inside are four keys, all different sizes.

"The organs with the smaller keys will be easier to open," she says.

I take the smallest key, enter my body and, eventually, find the lock to my liver. When I turn the key, my liver lights up so I can turn off my miner's light.

I come back out for air and another key, then go back down again and locate my kidneys. She has given me a roadmap. Again, when I turn the key, my kidneys light up—and my whole abdominal cavity is illuminated.

The second largest key is for my brain. Because the water stops at my throat, I can breathe. I have trouble finding the lock among all the creases. Eventually, I find it; when my brain lights up, it is beautiful and mysterious. Shadows and interesting shapes and designs keep me occupied for some time.

I leave to get the biggest and heaviest key—the key to my heart. Again, I have to hold my breath to dive into the water, now illuminated by my liver and kidneys. I find the lock, put in the key, and try to turn it. No luck. I come to the surface, gasping for air.

"You are trying too hard. You just have to turn the key gently," she says.

I go back down again, turn the key gently, and my heart lights up in a dazzling array of sparkling light. I am awed and overcome.

"Put this small box of keys back where you found it so you can unlock your Soul whenever you need," she says.

I thank her and continue down the road. I come upon two girls and ask them what is ahead.

"A small town," they say. Then with a gasp, "Did you see the crazy man and lady?"

"I met a man and a woman," I answer.

"Weren't you scared?"

"No, they helped me."

"Well, they are not normal. All of us try to avoid them," the girls tell me.

I continue along and see my "musical band" again—the dolphin, the hippo, the snake, and the chickadee. I walk through a door of the monastery and meet my guide. He greets me with open arms, and we hug. We walk to the bench and admire the view. I again see the shining box of love letters in the distant view.

Two monks come up and say we must be hungry. They hand each of us a bloodroot. It looks like a carrot with the coloring and texture of a beet. I bite into it, and blood-red juices drip down my mouth. It tastes so good.

My Interpretation

The musicians are wildlife that span water, land, and air—and they are from the mammal, bird, and reptile families. They draw me out of my usual thinking that only humans make music this beautiful. I am completely enveloped by the music around me; the animals are connected, unconditionally trusting, and harmonious.

I use my intuition to determine which road to travel. I calm my mind to *feel* guidance through my body. Now that my throat chakra has been opened by my eagle guide (see "My Eagle's Spirit Breath"), I am led to hear and speak Truth. I am guided down a path where I encounter two new guides who teach me this communication with my Higher Self.

The old man dislodges my blocks so I am able to listen to my Soul. In previous meditations (see "The City of Gold," "Painting our Self-Portrait," "Wanted" and "Cleansed of My Gold"), I endured great pain as my head felt like it was being ripped off. Now my old man literally takes off my head. This is the second time that my head has detached from my body. In the first (see "Painting our Self-Portrait"), my head and arm levitated and detached from my body when my monk guide touched my arm, and I lost the sense of being a body.

My old man dislodges a marble so large that it has completely closed off all avenues of communication. With these marbles, I have been blocking hearing God's Will. Our ego will does not give up easily; its tenacity for control is seemingly endless. The old man tells me I need to be vigilant to detect and dislodge these marbles as they form. As I become more aware of them, I can see my progress in being able to listen to God's Will. The old man's words strike such a chord with me. I am aware of being unable to speak from my heart. Someone helping me, someone *seeing* my pain—for I felt I had been able to keep it hidden—moves me to tears.

Now that I am unblocked, open, what does my Higher Self want to say? The old woman teaches me that I have the keys within me to access my Soul, to know what I want and how to say it from my heart.

The keys have always been there, but they have been hidden by the self that believes it is separate from everything and everyone.

I have four keys; three of them unlock organs that are surrounded by water, symbolically Universal Source Energy or "That Which is Everything." Only my brain is outside of this water, external to this Source Energy.

The first key unlocks my liver. Louise Hay's *You Can Heal Your Life* tells us that the liver is the "seat of anger and primitive emotions" (Hay, 1999, 203). I must unlock my anger, fear, and sadness and open love, joy, and happiness. I must look directly at the anger I hold, the anger that justifies my victimhood. Opening up my liver illuminates my torso, and I no longer need my miner's light. My path is made easier; the Light of my Soul is now visible.

The second small key unlocks my kidneys, which, according to *You Can Heal Your Life*, revolve around "criticism, disappointment, failure. Shame. Reacting like a little kid" (Hay, 1999, 202). I also need to explore my low self-worth in order to know my Self-worth. In doing so, the light grows stronger, the way to my heart clearer.

From here, the third key takes me to my brain. It is my ego-control system. I see it as beautiful. I honor my ego with its wonders, but I also do not understand it. It is mysterious, a word that evokes the idea of secrecy, falsehood. My brain keeps me preoccupied with shadows, shapes, and designs—to-do lists, worries, and concerns—none of which further my awareness. They only delay and sidetrack my journey to my Soul.

The way to open our heart is through seeing our life, and its sorrow, with gentleness—with non-judgment. In approaching ourselves with genuine gentleness when we dive into our "Soul's water," we easily unlock our hearts and experience a "dazzling array of sparkling light." It is through opening our hearts that we learn what is God's Will for us, what we truly want—to live the Love that we are.

Almost as an aside at the end of the meditation, two monks hand me a bloodroot. Before this meditation, I had no idea what a bloodroot was—or even that there was such a thing. When I discover that it is flower with a root as described in the meditation, I have a "knowing" sensation throughout my body that I am with Spirit. The root of the bloodroot is tubular; the sap inside appears like blood when the root is broken—it even coagulates like blood. It is a very powerful plant medicine used largely by Native Americans in the Lake Superior region—exactly where I live. These synchronicities fill me with awe.

How Do We Bring This into Our Lives?

Everything around us calls to us to *become* the resonance, the music, of the Universe. We need to observe what surrounds us and lose the fear that it appears different than our beliefs. If we can change our thinking about what "must be," we can begin to see "what is."

We receive guidance in many ways, including sensations in our body. We *know*. Such intuition gives us valuable information for what is in our best interest, and ultimately, the best interest of others. We need to heed our intuition—not diminish it.

Just knowing that we already have all the keys, have everything we need to unlock our Soul, is a huge step in moving toward picking up those keys and inserting them in the locks. We have to believe that we will find our keys. We all have keys to our heart and brain; whether we have the same number of other keys or have keys for the same organs does not matter. It only matters that we listen for guidance to find our keys—and for guidance to open the locks.

When we are living in our brain, our ego mind, we believe that we might drown if we enter and explore the "water" of our Soul. We think we will die. This process of discovery may be difficult. However, if we only deal with our issues in our brain, we are merely addressing them intellectually; we are still being guided by our ego. Going within, losing ourselves as we know us, can be very frightening. Unfortunately, this fear is most often taught; as very young children, we are not fearful. We can choose not to be fearful; we can choose to dive in with confidence that we have the keys, a roadmap, and a miner's lamp for our initial journey. For most of us, this process of living in our heart will require diving down with our keys many times, but the more we explore our Soul, the more confidently we dive in. We *will* die an ego death when we stay in the Universal "water." All will be illuminated, dazzling, and sparkling.

Our heart is the organ we often protect the most; in doing so, it can harden. With a gentleness and willingness to dive down, we can unlock our Soul's organ, the heart. If we are not gentle with ourselves, we cannot open the lock. We feel unworthy of opening it. After our attempts at doing so, we return to our brain, our ego, defeated and out of breath. It is not until we dive down with non-judgment that we can truly know what our Higher Self wants of us—and for us—so we can speak our true needs and wants from our Soul.

Why am I given a bloodroot? It is often used in the treatment of skin ailments. Perhaps I may need this medicine at some point—or perhaps you may.

My Heart's Secret Garden

∞

April 9, 2002

I am resting comfortably against a log on Driftwood Beach. I begin my meditation by asking myself, "What do I want?"

> "You need to go into your heart to find the answer," I hear.
>
> I take the key to my heart and dive down to open the lock. My heart is shimmering in dazzling light. I open it and step inside. I am in an antechamber with hundreds of bells ringing. There is no one pulling the cord, and I discover that they ring with the movement of my blood, moving in and out of my heart through my arteries and veins. I can hear the swish, swish.

I open the door to a room and see a long hallway, like a museum, filled with beautiful gowns displayed in glass cases.

"Have I worn these gowns?" I ask.

"Yes, some of them," I hear.

Through another door is the sewing room. Rows of women are sewing dresses that I presume will be for the hallway of gowns.

Through the next door, I see a large banquet table and large portraits on the wall. I am admiring it when, suddenly, the room comes to life with a banquet in progress. The time is the eighteenth century; the men and women are dressed up in the gowns from the hallway.

I watch a clearly important, handsome couple parade in. But then *I* am the lady. When we arrive at the table, my husband joins the men at the far end of the table. I stay with the women at the opposite end. The men engage in laughter and boisterous talk. We ladies are demure. I am not feeling connected to anyone in the room except for a quiet man sitting next to me. I wonder why he is not with the other men. He asks me to dance, but I decline. He tells me that it will be fine because everyone thinks he is homosexual. We dance and thoroughly enjoy each other.

The next day, I go into a secret, beautiful garden. I walk along a pathway and feel very peaceful. At the end of this path is my dance partner.

"Everyone has male and female in them, but right now your female energy is overpowering. You need to re-balance with your male side," he says.

He hugs me, and I can feel and see the energy passing between us. He tells me to crawl through the bushes to get a drink. I get on my hands and knees and come upon a pond. I lean over to get a drink and see my reflection in the water. I am beautiful; glowing lights dance around my head.

I drink the water and feel it surge through my body. It feels so wonderful that I take off my clothes and swim across the pond, feeling its warmth and strength. A hawk picks up my clothes and flies them across to me. I dress and walk in the meadow to the door to exit my heart. I step outside and lock it with the key.

My heart is aglow, and there are fireworks all around.

My Interpretation

What do I want? The answer is in my heart—shimmering and exploding with the joy of fireworks and celebration. I want balance in my energies. I want wholeness. The banquet, with the disconnection of the men and women—in distance and in behavior—reflects my imbalance. My guide in this meditation is a male who is the only one in the room I connect with. He looks male, but everyone thinks he is female. His energies are balanced, and no one "fears" him. He tells me that my female energy is overpowering—even though my female demeanor and subservience at the banquet appear weaker.

What is female energy? What is male energy? What does it mean to balance our male and female energies? When I first had this meditation, I thought that the male and female energies related to how we were acting, how we were interacting with the opposite sex, and how happy we were. I began to understand it more in the context of the characteristics of each sex. Women are more intuitive and nurturing; men are more logical and action-orientated. I still did not grasp how this translated into being both male and female.

I now understand the lesson of our male and female energies as two poles in our body, symbolized by the male-female harmony of my dance partner. One pole is the material world, and the other is the Spirit world. Our seven chakras or energy centers run along our spine from its base at the root chakra to the top of our head at the crown chakra. Our female pole is at the root chakra. This is the creation of the material world. The male pole is at the crown chakra. It is pure consciousness. As these two energies unite and balance, we transcend our bodies and become our Self. We merge, and know, our True Self in this world—and in the world of pure energy.

My female energy is overpowering; I am operating too much in this world of duality, this world of matter. When I dance with my "male side," both "poles" are united. I am happy. It is after I have danced with my male side that I enter a secret garden of my heart. It was secret from me because I was not balanced and open. When I look at myself in the Water of the Divine, I see my radiance, my glowing Essence, my Wholeness. When I drink It, the energy surges through my body. When I enter this Water naked, I fully commune with It. All of my possessions of this world are stripped away—my clothing, attitudes, and discontent. I bathe in the warmth and strength of Divine Water. Within my heart is my strength and comfort.

How Do We Bring This into Our Lives?

When we feel disconnected with others, whether they are the opposite gender or even the same gender, it may reflect an imbalance of our male and female energies. We *are* all One, but we are in a male or female body. Our outward appearance, mannerisms, way of thinking, strengths, and weaknesses may well create the illusion that we are one or the other, but from an energy perspective, we are a balance of both genders. This balance is important to our own well-being, but also for the well-being of society. In balancing our own personal male and female energies, we are able to approach the outside world from a place of self-acceptance and love—and the outside world will begin to change as well.

When we see ourselves as Divine Beings, the world of duality falls away. The concept of a differentiation between male and female disappears. It is replaced by the understanding that, while our physical characteristics are different and our inherent thinking patterns are often different, Who we are is completely undifferentiated. By awakening our creative energies in the material world and the world of Spirit, we are complete.

My Miracle of a Dove

∞

April 10, 2002

I have a Reiki treatment in the morning.

> I meet my guide at the gate of a white picket fence that swings inward to the garden surrounding the monastery. The beautiful garden has many white dogwoods, a few tall flowers, and the occasional tree.
> "Do you want to walk straight through the garden rather than on the pathway?" he asks.
> "I don't want to step on the flowers," I reply.
> "We don't have to," he says and pulls aside some flowers to reveal stepping stones.
> We proceed, stopping each time until he uncovers the next stepping stone. When we are in the middle of the garden, he asks if I'd like to sit down and meditate. We sit facing each other with our knees and hands

touching. The dogwoods around us begin to grow up and over us, creating a canopy. After a while, they return to their original shapes and sizes, except for one, which remains at about my face level.

"Eat it," my guide says.

"But I don't want to destroy it," I say.

"Eat just one petal," he says.

I eat one and wonder if I have eaten awareness, unity, universe, or understanding.

"Do you want to go into the monastery by the back door?" my guide asks.

"Yes."

We walk through the garden and reach an old wooden door that is partly covered in vines. It is locked, but he calls up to someone in a window overhead to come down and unlock the door.

The door creaks open. We enter a long tunnel-like hallway made of stone and lit only by torches on the walls. We walk along in silence and come upon a small room to the right. It is very Spartan; there is only a single bed with a white blanket, a night table, a book, and a candle. There is no window and no door.

"It looks rather dreary," I say.

"Some monks like to come down here to sleep where there is total silence and no disturbances. They have a small ruler to measure the candle so they know how long they've been here," he says.

We walk along further and come upon a similar room on the left. Then we arrive at an arched door, solid on the bottom with open latticework on the top. We open it and walk a short distance to a set of steep stairs. I climb up first and reach a trapdoor. I push it open and crawl out, only to find myself in the main room of the monastery. All of the monks are standing in a circle. They want me to dance since they know one of my dreams is to be a dancer. But I cannot dance. I am so embarrassed, I can't even move. One of the monks comes over and starts dancing with me to get me started, but I hold back and don't want to be the center of attention.

"Get me out of here," I plead to my guide.

He takes me to the bench, and I fall asleep.

When I awake, I find myself back in the monastery trying to dance. Still, I am completely unable to move.

My Reiki Master is now at my knees, and I think she might be able to get me moving.

"She cannot make you move. She can only help you when you are stumbling and need support."

I am outside of the monastery. I drag myself up, knowing that I must do this alone. I combine crawling, walking, and dragging myself to get to a log. There is someone ahead of me who is moving too slowly. I give them a push, and they fall over the log into a snowbank.

"Oh, sorry," I say.

I climb over the log into the deep snow. I am naked except for boots, but I am warm. I lift my feet high as I walk through the snow. I soon come upon a camel and wonder what he is doing in this cold climate. I mount him, and we walk along, eventually getting out of the snow.

In the afternoon, I go to Driftwood Beach. I lie down on the sand and lean against a cedar log that has recently drifted ashore. I marvel at its richly colored lines and "alive" smell. I relax and begin to meditate.

"Why did I seem to have such a short meditation this morning?" I ask my guide.

"First, you need to go through the colors," he says.

I first see red, flowing in waves rapidly outward. Then the movement stops, and red is calm. Then bright blue fills the screen of my vision.

"What is in the center?" he asks.

"A white circle," I answer.

He tells me to spin it. When I do, the circle elongates into a line. This line starts twirling around and moving throughout the blue in a clockwise direction and eventually settles. When I look at this newly created pattern, I see the white outline of a dove on a bright blue background.

I move to green and see an orange circle in the center. I go to turn it as well, but it won't move. I try counterclockwise, and it moves slightly. Then I see purple and, finally, white.

"Why was my meditation this morning shorter?" I ask again.

"You have had so many meditations this week. You need to be able to absorb and process their meaning. The subconscious is full of information, but it can't come too quickly. It needs to come through a funnel. Your funnel is getting backlogged, and you need to slow down the flow of information in order to receive a benefit. You have found inner peace and joy and know what they feel like. But sometimes, events and people will block that feeling. Just remember that you have found the feeling and remember to use it."

At the end of the meditation, I open my eyes. *Wouldn't it be wonderful if I saw a sign to show me that I wasn't making all of this up?*

No sooner have I thought this than a hawk flies right overhead.

What more do I need than this messenger as my sign? I walk back to the car, relaxed and at peace with this knowledge.

I have brought a friend's belated birthday gift with me and plan to drop it by her house on the way home. When I arrive, she has a gift for me as well; our birthdays are only a week apart. She hands me a beautifully papered, small, blue, rectangular box with a white angel over the domed top. I lift the lid and see a rock inside.

On one side of the rock is carved the exact dove of my meditation; on the other side is carved the word "Joy." I am speechless!

My Interpretation

I arrive at the monastery to meet my guide as usual. Instead of walking on the pathway through the garden, we uncover stepping stones and meditate together. We are enveloped in flowers; we *become* the garden rather than simply marveling at its beauty. My guide wants me to eat the dogwood, but concern—or fear—allows me to eat only one petal. As we are in the garden, I believe it is the first petal of awareness—learning to see into my Self and accepting and believing the lessons that are being given to me (see "Teachings of the Dogwood").

I am willing to follow the path before me—even if it presents challenges—but I am unable and/or unwilling to engage in what is asked of me at the end. I am completely paralyzed, both physically and physiologically, by being put to the test of following my dream of being a dancer. *Walking* the path to my Self I can manage; *becoming* my Self I cannot yet commit to. (I have since performed this dance in front of a large group of family and friends.) I presume that someone else will get me out of my paralysis. But not so. I must make the move; when I take this step, I will have all the help I need.

Who is this person that I push over the log? I apologize to them, but I do not help them up, see to them, or worry further. They represent the people or things that stand in our way of taking those steps to move out of our barrenness, the frigid world we live in when we are not living our True Nature. I will always be protected (here with my boots), but I am also naked of the things of this world. I am not cold, despite the fact that my mind tells me I should be; finally, I am taken out of the cold into the warmth.

My afternoon meditation still fills me with awe. Through focusing on colors, I am guided to draw the outline of a white dove. At the same time, I hear that I already know peace and joy. I know where to find them and what they feel like. I realize that my visions are profound, but I constantly question whether I am inventing them because I do not understand why I am experiencing them. I ask for proof—and miracles happen. I first receive the miracle of the hawk flying overhead. Hawk medicine is messenger. I am being given a message, a signal, that something is coming my way . . . my second miracle.

I receive this miracle as a birthday gift, a rock etched with the exact dove of my vision and the word "Joy" that I am told I know. My gift is housed in a treasure chest topped with an angel spreading her wings. Indeed, I receive a treasure—a direct answer from God.

This is one of the many miracles I am given over time to show me that I am truly experiencing these visions. However, despite them, I can assure you that it took many years for me to lose doubt that this was really happening.

What is the significance of the dove? In the Bible, the Book of Matthew tells us of the baptism of Jesus by John the Baptist:

> As soon as Jesus was baptized, he [*John the Baptist*] went up out of the water. At that moment heaven was opened, and he saw the Spirit of God descending like a dove and lighting on him [*Jesus*]. And a voice from heaven said, "This is my Son, whom I love; with him I am well pleased." (Matthew 3:16-17)

The dove is God, and He fills Jesus. God is within Jesus as He is within us. The dove has come to show me that God is within me. The dove is often thought of as a symbol of peace. In the story of Noah's Ark, the dove is the symbolic peace offering between God and mankind. I have been given the gift of awareness that I am One with God and that I will always be safe.

How Do We Bring This into Our Lives?

The garden at the monastery is a symbol of our Self. We can be awed by the beauty of the garden, even walk on one of its paths, but we need to venture *into* it so we can *be* our garden and not just *see* our garden. We need to lose our fear that we will harm it. Nothing we do will harm the garden of our Soul.

When we enter our garden (meditation is a good vehicle for this), we may feel paralyzed by what we are asked to do. Do we live the dreams that are within us? We need to remember that there is nothing we cannot do when asked by our Higher Self. When we are ready to take that first step, we will have all the help we need. When we think we are alone, when our mind tells us that we will be uncomfortable, we never are. We just need to ask for help from whichever Divine name resonates with us so we can begin to live the dreams that are within us.

Miracles are always showing us the Divine in our lives, but we often just do not see them or brush them off as coincidences, chance encounters, or lucky serendipity. These happenings are the messengers of Divine Intervention.

There is a treasure chest for each of us that contains a dove (a symbol of our Divinity) and the awareness of the joy that is ours. The treasure chest we seek is not laden with riches of this world but riches of our Self.

Once we become aware of our Divine Essence, we are hungry to be with It. However, we often need to absorb our learning before moving on to our next lesson. Otherwise, it may become more of an intellectual exercise. We need to learn at our own pace; lessons will come in their own time.

Meeting Jesus

∞

April 15, 2002

During my Reiki treatment, I am unable to get into meditation immediately.

> I ask my monk guide for help. He sits in front of me with his hands around my head. It helps, but every so often, I bring my outside life into my meditation.
>
> "Only half of your body is 'with' me. You need more help," he says.
>
> Jesus is beside him, looking exactly like the drawings from my Sunday school room. He is pouring water over my head.
>
> "I was already baptized as a child," I say.
>
> "When you are baptized as an adult, you understand what you are doing," he replies. "Look into my eyes."

I feel such peace and calm. He is sitting beside my guide, and I have an incredibly strong sense that I am sitting in the center of a circle of masters from all different beliefs. I can feel my eyes circling around in my head to look at the full group. I feel like they are all helping me.

Jesus says, "Look into the eyes of the master to your right."

I feel the same peace.

Jesus takes me into the Garden of Eden.

"Why didn't you allow Adam and Eve to enjoy all of the pleasures of this beautiful and bountiful garden? And why did you make Eve pick the fruit?" I ask.

"Adam picked a pear, but men wrote the reports," he answers. "Adam and Eve had the use of the fruits from all of the trees—except for one. They were happy and had all they needed, but greed, jealousy, and envy came over them, and they wanted it all. It was their undoing.

"Look at the two mountain peaks in the distance. The one on the left is happiness, and the one on the right is materialism. If you climb the happiness mountain, then the materialism mountain will superimpose upon it. You can enjoy the entire material world as long as you are climbing this mountain. However, if you start out on it, but get caught up in material things, you will switch over and be climbing the materialism mountain. And if you climb that mountain, the happiness mountain will remain distant and separate.

"Do you want to sit down on the bench?" he asks.

"Do you all have benches?" I ask.

"Yes," he replies.

When we arrive at the bench, I notice that it is for three people. The bench at the monastery is for two people.

"This bench is for the Father, the Son, and the Holy Spirit," he says.

I sit down in the middle with Jesus on my right and God on my left. God is a pulsating funnel of red light. I am in the Holy Spirit's position. I feel my head getting very, very hot as the Holy Spirit fills me.

My Reiki Master is at my head. When she moves to my shoulders, my head cools down.

Jesus and I walk down a path into Bethlehem. Ancient times soon become the modern day; there is terrible destruction and fighting all around.

"How can this be?" I ask.

Jesus answers, "The outside rim of the wagon wheel has broken, and people are falling off as they slide down the sides. The wagon wheel is broken on the bottom because the weight at the top is too much—too much poverty, conflict over oil, hatred, prejudice."

"But why now?" I ask.

"They have lost the flower on the top of the wheel. It has blown away. They need to find it," he replies. "But they will find it; it is only a matter of time."

We are still in Bethlehem, but now we are in Jesus' time. I see him giving a talk among a group of people. I join the circle and am overcome by his power and goodness. I feel so calm.

We go back to the bench, and I ask where the monastery is. He points to the right, telling me there is a bridge to it.

Since I know about bridges, I confidently walk over the edge—but I fall right down into the cavern. Fortunately, an eagle rescues me and flies me up.

"Why did that happen?" I ask, shocked.

"This bridge isn't like the other bridges. You have to know and learn where it is," Jesus says.

"Could you not just go and try every spot?" I ask.

"No," he says, "the eagle can only rescue you so many times. You have to understand where it is." He takes me across the bridge but stops half way.

"Are you not coming across?" I ask.

"You need to invite me."

I invite him to join me; on the other side, Jesus and my monk guide embrace. Light encircles them.

I say good-bye to Jesus and go to the bench at the monastery with my guide.

"I need to walk on one of the bridges," I say. I run out and land on a bridge. But suddenly, the bridge ends and I am dangling by one hand. "What happened?" I ask when he pulls me up to safety.

"You cannot just run out and expect to find a bridge. You must observe and notice what is around you in order to know the way. Otherwise, the bridges won't take you anywhere," he says.

My Interpretation

To date, I have considered my monk guide to be my primary teacher. Today, Jesus appears. He was the stranger who spoke with my monk guide in what to me was a foreign language, the language of love. He asked if he could sit on the bench with us (see "A Stranger"); in today's meditation, I need to invite him to join me. He will "be there" if we invite him.

Although I find Jesus' presence calming, I see him as the representative of Christianity, the church of my youth, and I have great difficulty with this, as I do not attend church, read the Bible, or feel any strong connection to the religion. I am unable to distinguish between the Christian doctrine and spirituality of the Christian faith. But beginning in this meditation, and for many to come, Jesus becomes a significant teacher for me.

Jesus appears because I need more help than my monk guide can provide. But I also have more help available to me. All the spiritual masters encircle me. Each one brings me peace. I am at the center of the wagon wheel, communing with all who come here from different paths.

Right from the moment we meet, I question Jesus. Firstly, should not he already know that I have been baptized! Jesus tells me that a baptism resulting from one's personal decision is done with conscious awareness, unlike an infant baptism.

I confront Jesus about Adam and Eve in the Garden of Eden, aggressively complaining and challenging him with unsaid, but real thoughts. *Why did you make Eve eat the apple and make her the evil one, the bad one, the temptress to innocent men? You are the cause of all of our patriarchal societies and the abuse against women. Why did you banish them from the Garden just because they made a minor mistake? Are you so unjust that we cannot be human in our frailties? It is your fault that we are unhappy.*

I hear Jesus' answer in the context of my thinking and interpret it as I assume it is said. "Adam picked a pear, but men wrote the reports." It is what I *want* to hear—that men are equally to blame for us being banished from the Garden, and that men writing the reports "proves" that we live in a patriarchal society. It does not answer why Adam and Eve were banished, but Jesus' response calms me down. It opens me up to hear him, to continue to listen, and be open to more lessons in the future so that, over time, I understand the stories in the Bible in a different way.

One such story is of Adam and Eve in the Garden of Eden. God created Adam from the dust of the earth and blew life, the Spirit, into him. God took Adam to the Garden of Eden to care for it and to be nourished by it. In the Garden were the Tree of Life and the Tree of Knowledge of Good and Evil. God told Adam that he could eat from any tree in the Garden except the Tree of Knowledge, for if he did he would die. God put Adam into a sleep and created Eve out of his rib. They lived happily in this Garden, not knowing they were naked, and so were not embarrassed by it. But the serpent told Eve of the wisdom she would have from eating from the Tree of Knowledge; she would become God when her eyes were opened to knowing good and evil. She ate a fruit and gave one to Adam. It was then that they saw their nakedness and were afraid of the Lord and covered themselves with fig leaves. God asked them who told them that they were naked, and realized that they must have eaten from the Tree of Knowledge. God told the serpent that hatred would exist between him and all else. God told Eve that she would have pain in childbearing and be beholden to her husband. To Adam, God said that all of his life, from birth to death, would be full of pain and toil. And then, as an even worse fate, God banished them from the Garden, where complete abundance and happiness abound (Genesis 2:4–25 and 3:1–24).

Taken literally, God seems like a vengeful God who wants to keep things from Adam and Eve and is quick to punish. Eve is responsible for first attracting the serpent to her, listening to it, and then eating the fruit. Adam is tempted by Eve and falls from Grace as a result. As Eve's penalty, she will be subservient to her husband and endure pain in childbirth. Adam's entire life will be sweat, toil, and tears. If it were not for Eve, we would all be fulfilled and happy.

How do I now understand this story? The Tree of Life is the Eternal Spirit, the Essence of Who we are. The Tree of Knowledge of Good and Evil is the concept of duality or this world of the body (our separate selves); this world of you/me, us/them, rich/poor, abundance/scarcity, war/peace, right/wrong, my God/your God, my side/your side, and so on. In the world of Spirit, there is no duality; all is One.

God breathes Himself into Adam. Adam is as God is. *A Course in Miracles* tells us that we can create as God created by extensions of ourselves. "To think like God is to share His certainty of what you are, and to create like Him is to share the perfect Love He shares

In the Beginning

with you" (*ACIM*, 1996, 113). Thus, Eve is created from Adam and not from God. Adam shared of his Self, figuratively his rib. We, too, can create by sharing our Self.

Before falling from Grace, Adam and Eve were naked in the Garden but did not notice, as they were part of the Oneness and not of the body. The serpent here is the ego. By eating of this Tree of Knowledge, by entering this world of duality, Adam and Eve left the Oneness, the Divine, and entered the world of the ego (the belief that the body is who we are, that we are separate from the Divine, and that we need to have all our neighbor has, and more). By seeing ourselves as part of this duality, we are no longer in the Garden of Eden; we see ourselves as naked, exposed to this difficult world.

And in this world, the ego with this hatred, judgment, and fear crushes our head and kicks our heels, just as God decreed. As a female, the process of childbearing is painful—and we live in a patriarchal society. For males, living in the world of body can very often be a toil, as God told Adam. If we are not connected to Spirit, our lives seem difficult. If we ingest, absorb, and take into ourselves the world of duality (the body), then our mind will believe it has been banished from the Garden, from heaven. When we live in Spirit, it is not that we will not face challenges, but we will see these challenges differently. We will see them through the eyes of vision.

How do I now interpret Jesus' answer? With an open heart, clear of ego assumptions and associations, I hear: "Adam picked a pair, but men (mankind) wrote the reports." With his own free will, Adam *chose* the world of duality—good/evil, male/female. He chose two—a pair—rather than One, and left the world of non-duality, left the Garden of Eden. In this world of duality, Adam and Eve saw their differences, their nakedness, and were embarrassed by it. "But men (mankind) wrote the reports." Mankind cannot see that it has made this choice. We do not remember being in the Garden—we have forgotten Who we are—and write the story from the perspective of this world of duality.

Once Jesus is able to calm my ego-anger toward him, I am able to hear the lesson of *intention* through the analogy of the mountains of happiness and materialism. When our true intention is to be happy, we will achieve happiness and experience great abundance in all forms. But an intention of getting bigger and better things, accolades, accomplishments, and money will not bring us the happiness we desire. Two people may have the same material things and look identical by any physical standard, but they could be completely different in their happiness and well-being.

The bench at the monastery has been a place of learning for me. Now I discover that each religion has its own bench, a place to sit with one's spiritual masters. In the Christian tradition, the Holy Trinity sits on its bench. God and Jesus surround me, and I am filled with the Holy Spirit and experience my Divine Being.

This is the first time that I am taken to Bethlehem. I see the comparison between the goodness of Jesus' preaching and the destruction of current time in 2002. The teaching of the wagon wheel continues. It is breaking under the burden from the loss of the flower. What is this flower? It is the dogwood flower embracing the teachings of awareness, unity, universe, and understanding (see "Teachings of the Dogwood"). It has not left, only blown away. We have just lost sight of it. We will find the flower; it is only a matter of time.

There will always be a bridge anywhere we *need* it, but there is not always a bridge where we *want* it to be. In all of my previous meditations, I have been led to trust in the existence of bridges, that they will span great valleys to get me to where I will learn, and that a bridge will always be there when I need it. In this meditation, my understanding of bridges has expanded from knowing that there will always be a bridge to a lesson that there are also bridges between the various belief systems, the various spokes of the wagon wheel. Walking on these bridges takes awareness of where this journey leads. These bridges are to be crossed when they are in our best interests, but unlike the other bridges, we need to understand what is at the other end before heading out.

I am taught that, while there are still all the bridges I need, I must be aware of where I am going, be observant of the path that I am on, and see the signs that direct me. Without this connection, there will be no meaning to them, we will not get anywhere, and we will just be taking bridges with no direction, passion, or steadfastness. We will be rescued when we fall, but in order to learn this, we will be rescued only so many times before we need to fall into the valley to wake up.

How Do We Bring This into Our Lives?

What path to the Truth do we follow? In order to truly engage in spiritual growth, whatever path we follow needs to be ours, to be what resonates and speaks to us. Often, but certainly not always, this tends to be the path of our birth. But one's path certainly does not need to be a traditional religion or the traditional path of that religion.

If we find that abundance is not coming to us, we are not climbing the happiness mountain—our happiness is not our mantra. This is not happiness that can be bought. It is happiness of being our Self and following our life purpose. We must not get caught up in abundance that comes our way on this happiness mountain; if it drags us over to the materialism mountain, happiness will start to elude us.

We can return to the Garden of Eden whenever we want, we just have to understand Who we are—our Higher Self as God created us. Within the Garden of Eden, there is total abundance. It is our choice—we can live in a world of our separate selves where we face scarcity or we can live in world of Spirit where we have everything we need and want.

At the Center of the Wagon Wheel

∞

April 24, 2002

During my Reiki treatment, the flute/piper music is playing.

As I am sitting listening to the music, a girl comes over and dresses me in a white robe and ivy garland. She gently pulls me up, and we walk until we arrive at a lattice archway entwined with ivy.

I step through by myself into what seems to be an observatory with a glass dome-shaped roof and mostly green plants around the outer edges. The middle is open with a smooth dirt floor. In the center, there is an asymmetrical plant sculpture. It has a rectangular base with one end much higher than the other and what looks like mountain peaks in between. In a large circle around this sculpture are numerous stone benches. I

Led by Grace

recognize two of them—one from the monastery and the other from the Christian mountain.

My guide appears and says, "Look at the sculpture from all of the benches."

I am expecting that, as I move around to each bench, this sculpture will appear as a new wonderful image. But no. The image is exactly the same, regardless of where I sit. There is no mirror image, no side image; all views are exactly the same. I can't understand this, and I walk up to the sculpture and peer over the top. It looks exactly as I would have expected.

My guide says, "Everyone is looking at exactly the same thing. They think they are different because of their vantage point. But it is the same.

"We are in the inner rings of the wagon wheel. No matter from what angle you approach, the final image is always the same. Here, we can see the other benches; on the outside, you don't want to see them."

"Why have I been brought to see this? I'm not so special," I say.

"That's right," he says. "You're not so special. You are like everyone else, but you found the path."

"What do my white gown and garland mean?" I ask.

"Your white gown is for pureness of thought. I will have to think about the garland," he answers.

I suspect he wants me to figure it out for myself.

"What happens if more than one person comes here at the same time?" I ask.

"That happens. The first time I was here, I thought I was alone, but there was someone else here. He saw me and realized I couldn't see him. So he sent me thoughts. Years later, the man came up to me in a market and told me he'd been with me. I now see other people if they are here," he says.

"Are there other people here now?" I ask, but he doesn't answer.

We can see that it is getting dark, and we head out of the garden. I realize that this is the first time in my meditations that it is nighttime. I see the beautiful night sky dancing with millions of stars.

"In the day, you use your sight to guide you, but at night, your other senses are much keener. This is when deeper understanding comes," he says.

I hear the night animals and play "blinking" games with an owl. This is how I imagine my night walk in Peru will be.

"I am going to Peru to hike the Inca Trail," I tell him.

"I know," he says, "and you will learn and understand something very special."

As I walk, my hands and forearms become increasingly heavy. It feels like they are encased in cement blocks. Even my tongue and neck feel heavy.

Dawn is approaching. I want to go to the monastery. It is then that I notice the garlands hanging from the trees and the gate of the monastery. I know what my garland meant—everything is connected and circular, continuous, universal, linked. I have such a sense of peace.

"Why was I given the garland?" I ask.

"Because you are special."

"But I thought you said that there was nothing special about me."

"I said that you are not so special," he says. "You are special, as is everyone else, but there is nothing more special about you. How people use their talents is up to them."

We walk into the monastery and stop by the columns. Etched on them are names of people who have been here before. I add my name with great care. We go to the bench, again in the darkness of night, and look upon the brilliance of the stars.

My Interpretation

I am taken to the asymmetrical plant sculpture at the center of the wagon wheel, symbolically God (however one names Him). It is housed in a glass dome. All is transparent and available. This dome distinguishes the world we live in from the world of Spirit. Access is through an archway of ivy and, before I enter, I am cloaked in a white robe for pureness of thought and an ivy garland on my crown chakra for the awareness of Oneness.

From other meditations, I am familiar with two of the benches circling the central plant sculpture. I am shown the benches of all of the spokes of the wagon wheel. The asymmetrical shape of the plant's sculpture suggests that it would look different from every bench, that "my God, my Divine" is different for every viewer. But when we walk around to each bench, the sculpture looks exactly the same; It never changes. How we name the center of this wheel—God, Universe, Source, Divine Essence, Jesus, Buddha, Krishna, Allah—may appear unique to us, but It appears the same regardless of name and regardless of which path is taken to It.

"I'm not so special," I state. The word "so" moves "special," meaning blessed, to an ego belief or statement from a spiritual one. "So special" involves comparison, "better than," "deserving," "judging." Everyone among us is the same Divine Essence of Love.

Nighttime offers a new sensation for me. We normally rely very heavily on our sight. We believe what we see with our eyes. But Truth lies not in what we see with our eyes but in the vision of our third eye.

How Do We Bring This into Our Lives?

All benches and all pathways to the Divine are visible when we are with our Self; we see everyone as One. We need to understand that no matter how "unique" *our* God is, how different we make Him or believe Him to be, that "All That Is" is One; the same One for all of us, no matter the route we take. And when we arrive at the center and believe that we are alone, we need to "learn" to be able to see others on different benches there with us, share with them, and create.

The language we use is important, and it is critical to be aware of our words and body language when the ego gets involved. One little word—*so*—transforms a Divine Truth of "I am special, blessed" into an ego stranglehold of "I am so special, better than others." We need to be aware of our word choices.

Chains of the Body, Freedom of the Soul

∞

May 8, 2002

With all that's been going on, I am not sure if I will be able to concentrate during my Reiki treatment. But I enter a deep state quickly.

> I am sitting on the bank of a grassy slope that leads to a dirt road. A line of religious scholars—men and women from all faiths—walks by very slowly. The music playing sounds so sad that I think it is a funeral march. But then the line changes to a string of chained prisoners trudging back to the prison with prison guards keeping watch. Their heads are bowed, and they kick up clouds of dust as they shuffle along. From time to time, one of the prisoners looks up at me. Then the line of religious scholars reappears. They are walking in step beside the prisoners, moving close to them, taking some of them

by the hand, and leading them away. The remaining prisoners continue on in a line to the left while the scholars and prisoners with them walk in a line to the right and around the bend. I can see the ends of their lines in the distance.

My guide comes by and asks if I want to take a walk.

"Why did the prison guards let those prisoners go?" I ask him.

"They didn't see them," he answers.

"Did they see me?"

"They *could* see you, but they chose not to. They are not yet aware enough to sense your presence. The prisoners who went with the scholars could see them; the others could not," he says.

"Are we on a different plane?" I ask.

"No," he says, "but we are here with a different energy."

"I want to sit for a while and enjoy the sunset," I say. "It is so peaceful."

"Look at your feet," my guide says. They are bare, but I don't see anything unusual at first. After a while, I notice that, although there is nothing wrong with them, they are a little dirty from the road.

"That is right," he says. "After all of your journeys, your feet have grown calluses to protect you from cuts or sores. You will be safe along your way. May I clean your feet?" He cleans my feet and they feel so warm.

My feet and legs feel so heavy that I have trouble when I start to walk. My guide brings me a "vehicle," somewhat like a recumbent bicycle, but it moves along a rail track. It feels very relaxing until we arrive at a large downhill. I am terrified as I fly down the hill. At the bottom, there is a funny smell. I drag myself back up the steep hill and meet my guide at the top.

"I had no control," I complain.

"You have full control; you are in total control of yourself. You just have to move your body and the 'car' will go where you want and at the right speed," he says.

I get back on, but I am unable to move my legs or arms. It is nighttime, and I can see the eyes of the owls, the lynx, and every other woodland creature. I know with certainty that this is where I am supposed to be. I have no fear and feel so peaceful. It is very quiet.

Then dawn starts to break and, amazingly, the music gets louder as the wildlife wakes up to this beautiful day. I can hear the birds and the squirrels. It is like nature's symphony. I am becoming hungry and thirsty. I bend over to get some water from a brook and notice a frog drinking. I pick berries and notice a bird eating them beside me. I realize the frog and the bird will keep me safe and are telling me that it is all right to drink this water and eat these berries.

My Interpretation

The religious scholars represent the various pathways to our Self, the various pathways to the center of the wagon wheel. This may or may not be traditional religion; it is any path that brings us back to Who we are. The prisoners represent our ego belief that we are our bodies. Everything seems slow. Moving outward from the energy of our physical body are our emotional, mental, and spiritual bodies. The vibrational energy of the physical body, the densest of all of our bodies, is slow.

The line of religious scholars changes to a line of bedraggled, chained prisoners who have toiled all day long, just as God told Adam that he must toil for the rest of his life. That is not to say that life is always dreary—that there are never moments of happiness and joy—but they are fleeting and can easily be wiped away by experiences and factors outside of us. As believers in our separateness—as believers that we are our bodies—we are connected to one another, not by the joy of knowing our Oneness, but by shackles against our will. We create clouds of dust that blur our vision.

As we become aware of our Divinity and open up to the possibility and probability of our Higher Self, we begin to enter a different energy. We are able to recognize the guides who will lead us down our spokes to the center of the wagon wheel.

My feet have become dirty, yet completely protected, as I have walked along my journey. For the first time in my meditations, my feet are washed, and my legs and arms become immobile. I am losing the concept of self as a body, as we begin to do when we leave the prisoner line and join with our "religious scholar," our guide. We are given a different means for going through life, a "vehicle" we completely control. But we must learn, we must *understand,* that we are in full control. For without this understanding, even with our new "vehicle," life's challenges will seem terrifying. Not only will they be terrifying, there may be a "bad smell" at the end; something is not right. We are intellectually aware of our Higher Self, but we have not internalized it. When we *live* our Higher Self, we control where we go and at what speed we travel. We create our lives as we want.

The concept of night returns in this meditation. Day and night are not light and dark in terms of good and evil—but rather in terms of which eyes we use to see. At night, we see with the vision of our third eye, with God-Awareness. I know with certainty that this is where I am to be.

When I return to daylight, to this world of using our eyes, I hunger and thirst. The Beatitudes speak of this: "Blessed are those who hunger and thirst for righteousness, for they will be filled" (Matthew 5:6). I seek nourishment for my Soul, to be with this God-Awareness when in body. The frog and the bird guide me to such nourishment so that I will be filled with Grace.

How Do We Bring This into Our Lives?

We need to notice the people, events, things that jar us, tug at us to look up and veer off of the prisoners' path we are on. We may begin to hear a spirit guide; a series of serendipitous events may awaken us to messages and guidance from outside of our traditional thoughts; we may experience a job loss, a job offer, a troubled relationship, a new relationship, or an unexpected gift of some kind. Whether we consider them positive or negative, these situations help clear the cloud of dust surrounding our ego-based lives. We need to listen to such guidance if it resonates with our Soul—if it speaks to us and fills us with a peaceful power. We need to free ourselves from our prisoner chains. There is no need to be captive to fear or worry.

We are in control; we determine our lives. With this understanding, we are able to move through life creating all that we desire. For many of us, this understanding seems "beyond" us. We might begin by seeing our "vehicle of Grace" as the means to ride through our life with control—not of events that happen outside us, not with control of others—but at least with the ability to more easily move through the difficult situations that life presents. With this start, and the faith that results, we begin to understand that we *are* creating our life.

Answering the Call

∞

May 15, 2002

When my Reiki treatment begins, I don't seem to have a clear direction—just flashes of images. I feel as if I am wandering with no sense of direction. Eventually, I am able to focus.

> I am walking along a scenic road with deciduous trees overhanging the road like an umbrella. I see many people sitting in pews along the road. The music sounds sad, and I think that perhaps this is my funeral. I feel a small pain behind my right eye and wonder if I have a brain tumor. Although I feel like I am walking down the aisle, I question whether I am actually in a coffin.
>
> Jesus and my monk guide meet me, extending their arms and bringing me down from my observer's viewpoint.
>
> "You need some guidance," they say.

"I can't keep a set image. I am all over the place."

They suggest that we walk, but I can't because my legs are so heavy. Then my whole body is heavy.

"Let's leave our bodies," they suggest.

I'm not quite ready for that, but I concentrate and go deeper. My body is so heavy.

"Bring your soul up from your toes, up through your body and blow it out your mouth," they say.

I blow my soul out as a white puff of smoke. Jesus and my monk do the same: one is red, the other blue. I look down and see our motionless bodies standing together in a circle.

Our souls take off and regain form as children in a playground. We are carefree—laughing, running, playing tag and hopscotch. Then we go to the swings, Jesus on one side of me, my monk on the other.

"Let's jump off," I say.

We are so high that it is scary. A lake appears for us to jump into. I am still frightened, but I jump off and sink to the bottom of the lake. I clamor out with the help of my guides, but I am still scared.

We go climb ropes. Again Jesus and my monk are on either side. I become afraid about halfway up.

"There's no one below to catch me if I fall," I say.

They say, "Don't fall."

"But what if I accidentally fall?"

"Don't accidentally fall," they reply.

"But I need a hand; I need you to help me," I say.

"Why do you need us to push you up when you're out of your physical body?" they ask.

I then know that I can make it and begin climbing up slowly and carefully.

At the top ledge, I rest with my guides and look up at the sky. The night sky is lit with millions of brilliant stars. I turn and notice that the other half of the sky is a beautiful day sky.

"It would be easy to fall off the edge," I say.

"Just don't fall," they answer.

"But what if you fall accidentally?"

"You cannot fall accidentally. You can only slip, and this is a choice. If you slip, you have decided which way you want to go," they say.

The phone rings three times in my Reiki Master's office. But it continues to ring in my meditation.

I stand up and see a cloudy passage as the phone continues to ring. As I look for the phone, I enter the white cloud. I can't see anything, but I follow the sound of the ring. I find the phone and say, "Hello." It is God on the other end. He talks for a while, but I just stammer and don't say much. We say good-bye, and I rejoin my guides.

"It was God on the phone, but I didn't have anything profound to say," I tell them, quite upset with myself.

"At least you answered the phone. Many people don't answer it—and most don't even hear it," they say.

We return to our bodies.

The entire time that I am out of my body, I have pain in my right hip, my neck, and behind my right eye. When I go back into my body, the pains are gone.

I find myself walking along the same road as in the beginning of the meditation. The people are smiling, the music is happy, and I feel good. I am walking in the opposite direction.

I am by myself. The music has stopped completely. I slowly walk along in silence, and then I look up and see a "hole" in the sky. Beams of light radiate down to me.

The music starts again, very joyous music, and the light beams fill me and pulsate back and forth between this "hole" in the sky and me. I am connected to God.

My Interpretation

This is a lesson in the death of the ego and the reconnection with our Divine Essence. My "funeral" for the ego takes place in what is to become my sacred forest of deciduous trees, the place where so much of my future learning takes place. Deciduous trees have the appearance of death every fall and of rebirth every spring, all the while being fully alive.

Jesus and my monk take me on an out-of-body experience. My Essence appears as a white puff of smoke, the color of the crown chakra and the connection with the Divine. However, Jesus and my monk's Essences are red and blue. Red is the color of the first chakra, the root chakra, and is the color that often makes me feel agitated. Blue is the color of the fifth chakra, the throat chakra, where I experienced significant pain as my head felt as though it was being ripped off. Their Essences *appear* as red and blue to help heal my blocked chakras.

We "re-form" as happy, carefree children—an age where we may still be aware of our connection to our Divine Self. But the swings and climbing the ropes create fear; moving beyond my comfort zone is frightening. I have vivid memories of climbing a waterfall in my late twenties and becoming paralyzed when I could not reach the next handhold. Eventually, I committed to moving up, but I was shaking all over. Fears from the past need not affect the present. I am taught that I will always be safe in my landings and that there will be help for me. My Higher Self has the ability to "climb any mountain." I can do it myself when I am in my Essence.

At the top of my difficult climb, I see the beauty of the light and the dark. I see that they are not in competition, but fully brilliant and beautiful in themselves. I think about how easy it would be to fall from such a place of Grace. But to leave here is a choice. We can choose to stay in this place even while in the body.

God is calling. I can hear the call and follow it. I am so surprised to be hearing from God that I cannot speak, and I cannot remember what He says. I am upset with myself for not being more profound and articulate. I wanted to impress God; my ego still has a strong presence. Most important, I hear the call and answer it—a step in the right direction to knowing my Self.

When I return to my physical body, my aches and pain have disappeared. Everything in my sacred forest is joyous: the people are smiling, the music is happy, and I feel good. I am then alone, and I see and experience my direct connection with God. I answered His call. In time, I will be able to hear His words and speak mine. I am given the *feeling* of being truly alive while in my body.

How Do We Bring This into Our Lives?

We always have a choice. It may not appear so, but whatever happens in our lives is a choice we have made—perhaps not with complete consciousness, but *we* made it. And as such, we can *choose* to be with our Higher Self.

Do we hear the call? Do we answer it? The call may appear as a conversation, a feeling, a knowing, an intuition, or a passion. It is something that lightens our Soul, drives us to follow the message, and leads us to peace and happiness. What is bothering us disappears; what enlightens us takes its place. It is through listening for the call, and answering it, that we receive direct communication from God.

Afterword

This is only the beginning, but the start is glorious.

In one of my first meditations, I saw myself as two people: an extremely sad-looking female and a smiling, welcoming, energetic male. How I presented myself to the world differed from my internal lack of peace. I did not know Who I was. Through parables, I have been taught lessons along my journey that will lead me to finding my Self. I have been taught to trust, to see the Love that I am, to use my intuition, to realize there are bridges that shorten this journey and take me to a lesson, to change my perspective on what is valuable, and to follow my guides—in whatever forms they take. With them, I have grown to hear God's call—and I have answered it. By doing so, I have become directly connected to God, infused with radiant light—even though I cannot yet hear what He says.

You may resonate with my interpretations—or you may understand the lessons in a different way. It does not matter. What matters is that these visions draw you into thinking about Who you are. And perhaps they lead to discussions with others.

We are a shining light, one that completes a brilliant constellation in the sky. Without us shining forth, the story of that constellation will not be seen or told. I hope that, with reading this book, you will know your brilliance, and understand your part as one of the whole, individual in appearance but the same in your Essence.

Until the next book in *Led by Grace*...

Acknowledgments

I am so very grateful for the blessings in my life, which were always there but not always visible to me.

I am blessed with my four children in so many ways. As your parent, you gave me unconditional love and the opportunity to learn from my mistakes, to break patterns, and to teach new ways of thinking.

I am thankful for my loving, caring, and supportive family. My relationship with each of you is stronger and more intimate than ever, and I cherish every moment.

Life becomes even richer when we have intimate friendships. I am blessed to have friends with whom my life, my feelings, my beliefs, and my trials are an open book. I thank you all.

I extend my gratitude to Anna Marie Bougie for introducing me to Reiki. You brought me to the door leading to my Self.

I thank my editor, Dennis Denomy. Your ease with language and thoughtful questions helped create a polished manuscript.

Although I have read many books that have brought me closer to awareness of my Self, *A Course in Miracles* has been one of the most influential. It has complemented my visions and allowed me to see them in a different light.

Finally, I am so very grateful to you, the reader. For without the need to share my experiences through writing my story, I would not have studied and contemplated my journals. Re-experiencing my journey has further transformed my life . . . and I hope it has transformed yours.

Permissions

Grateful acknowledgement is made for permission to reprint excerpts and a map from the following copyrights:

Anatomy of the Spirit: The Seven Stages of Power and Healing, Caroline Myss, 1996. Reprinted by permission of Three Rivers Press.

A Handbook of Chakra Healing: Spiritual Practice for Health, Harmony, and Inner Peace, Kalashatra Govinda, 2004. Reprinted by permission of Konecky and Konecky.

Lake Superior Provincial Park map reprinted by permission of Lake Superior Provincial Park, Wawa, Ontario. Adaptation of this map by Daniel Klassen Graphics for *Led by Grace,* printed by permission.

Medicine Cards, Jamie Sams and David Carson, 1999. All rights reserved. Reprinted by permission of St. Martin's Press, New York.

You Can Heal Your Life, Louise L. Hay, 1999. Reprinted by permission of Hay House, Inc., Carlsbad, California.

SELECTED BIBLIOGRAPHY

A Course in Miracles: Text, Workbook for Students, Manual for Teachers. Mill Valley, California: Foundation for Inner Peace, 1996.

Dalai Lama. *The Good Heart: A Buddhist Perspective on the Teachings of Jesus.* Somerville, Massachusetts: Wisdom Publications, 1996.

———. *An Open Heart: Practicing Compassion in Everyday Life.* New York: Back Bay Books, 2002.

Dyer, Wayne W. *Change Your Thoughts—Change Your Life: Living the Wisdom of the Tao.* Carlsbad, California: Hay House, 2007.

———. *The Power of Intention.* Carlsbad, California: Hay House, 2005.

———. *WISHES Fulfilled: Mastering the Art of Manifesting.* Carlsbad, California: Hay House, 2012.

Einstein, Albert. *Physics and Reality.* www.kostic.nlu.edu, 1936.

Fox, Emmet. *Sermon on the Mount: The Key to Success in Life.* New York: HarperOne, 1989.

Govinda, Kalashatra. *A Handbook of Chakra Healing: Spiritual Practice for Health, Harmony, and Inner Peace.* Old Saybrook, Connecticut: Konecky and Konecky, 2004.

Hawkins, David R. *The Eye of the I.* W. Sedona, Arizona: Veritas Publishing, 2001.

———. *I: Reality and Subjectivity.* West Sedona, Arizona: Veritas Publishing, 2003.

———. *Power vs. Force: The Hidden Determinants of Human Behavior.* Carlsbad, California: Hay House, 2002.

Hay, Louise L. *You Can Heal Your Life.* Carlsberg, California: Hay House, 1999.

Holden, Robert. *Shift Happens!: How to Live an Inspired Life … Starting Right Now!* Carlsbad, California: Hay House, 2011.

The Holy Bible: New International Version. Colorado Springs, Colorado: International Bible Society, 1984.

Lerner, Harriet. *The Dance of Anger: A Woman's Guide to Changing the Patterns of Intimate Relationships.* New York: Harper and Row, 1985.

Myss, Caroline. *Anatomy of the Spirit: The Seven Stages of Power and Healing.* New York: Three Rivers Press, 1996.

Pagels, Elaine. *The Gnostic Gospels.* New York: Vintage Books, 1989.

Ruiz, Don Miguel. *The Four Agreements.* San Rafael, California: Amber-Allen Publishing, 1997.

——. *The Mastery of Love.* San Rafael, California: Amber-Allen Publishing, 1999.

Sams, Jamie and David Carson. *Medicine Cards.* New York: St. Martin's Press, 1999.

Tolle, Eckhart. *The Power of Now: A Guide to Spiritual Enlightenment.* Novato, California: New World Library, 1999.

Williamson, Marianne. *A Return to Love: Reflections on the Principles of A Course in Miracles.* New York: Harper Paperbacks, 1993.

Yogananda, Paramahansa. *Autobiography of a Yogi.* Los Angeles, California: Self-Realization Fellowship, 2001.

About the Author

Writing is Sandra's third career. Her first was in the investment industry, where she became a director and senior investment analyst for a major international firm. Her second was as a full-time mom of four children. These careers helped provide the skills and space to nurture this latest chapter of her life.

Sandra lives in Wawa, Ontario, where she spends much of her time in the pristine natural environment. Her day begins with meditation and yoga.